Local Tax Policy

David Brunori

Other Urban Institute Press Titles by David Brunori
State Tax Policy: A Political Perspective
The Future of State Taxation

Local Tax Policy

A Federalist Perspective

THE URBAN INSTITUTE PRESS
WASHINGTON, DC

THE URBAN INSTITUTE PRESS
2100 M Street, N.W.
Washington, D.C. 20037

Library of Congress Cataloging in Publication Data

Brunori, David.
    Local tax policy: a federalist perspective / David Brunori.
        p. cm.
    Includes bibliographical references and index.
    ISBN 0-87766-717-9 (alk. paper)
    1. Local taxation—United States. 2. Local finance—United States.
3. Intergovernmental fiscal relations—United States. I. Title.
    HJ2385.B775 2003
    336'.01473—dc22
                                                     2003015145

Printed in the United States of America

THE URBAN INSTITUTE is a nonprofit, nonpartisan policy research and educational organization established in Washington, D.C., in 1968. Its staff investigates the social, economic, and governance problems confronting the nation and evaluates the public and private means to alleviate them. The Institute disseminates its research findings through publications, its Web site, the media, seminars, and forums.

Through work that ranges from broad conceptual studies to administrative and technical assistance, Institute researchers contribute to the stock of knowledge available to guide decisionmaking in the public interest.

Conclusions or opinions expressed in Institute publications are those of the authors and do not necessarily reflect the views of officers or trustees of the Institute, advisory groups, or any organizations that provide financial support to the Institute.

This book is dedicated to
Larry Kelberg
who took a piece of our hearts with him.

Contents

Acknowledgments

I completed this book while serving as a David C. Lincoln Fellow at the Lincoln Institute of Land Policy. The book would have been impossible to complete without the financial support of the Institute. Few organizations are as influential in the field of public finance and it has been a privilege to be affiliated with the Institute. I owe a particular debt of gratitude to Joan Youngman, senior fellow at the Institute. She is not only a renowned scholar, but also one of the nicest people I have ever had the pleasure of knowing. Her encouragement and support were invaluable. I would like to thank Chris Bergin, executive director of Tax Analysts. I have had the honor to work for Tax Analysts most of my professional career. It is an organization that encourages, indeed inspires, its employees to think critically about tax policy. This is my third book with the Urban Institute Press, and I cannot say enough about its staff. Rick Custer, Scott Forrey, Glenn Popson, and Fiona Blackshaw epitomize professionalism and dedication. I am very proud of my association with the Press and its staff. Finally, nothing would be possible without my wife, Elisse Brunori. I owe everything to her.

All failings you may find in this book are mine and should not be attributed to the editors or reviewers.

1

Introduction

But where will we get the money?
> —Township mayor in testimony before state legislative committee, 2001

The above quote captures the attitude of many local public officials. Local governments across the United States are struggling to raise revenue to pay for public services. Increased demands by citizens for more, and better, public services; the ever-rising costs of providing services; and a plethora of legal and political restrictions on raising tax revenue have left many American local governments in dire fiscal straits. These revenue problems are not the result of economic downturn. Rather, the problems stem from structural deficiencies that pose a risk to raising revenue and meeting government service responsibilities far into the future.

The ongoing fiscal problems have prompted much discussion in recent years about the future of local government finance. Scholars, government leaders, and representatives of a wide variety of organizations have been debating how local governments will continue to pay for public services (for example, see Ladd 1998; Oates 2001b; Peterson 1994; Swartz and Bonello 1993; Woodwell 1998). The increased discussion, and the prominence of the discussants, illustrates the importance of local governments in the United States and the services they provide.

The goal of this book is to examine how local governments are financed with an eye toward their current and future responsibilities within the American federal system.[1] The hypothesis of this book is relatively simple:

The existence of local government that Americans are familiar with will be in jeopardy without a significant change in the way local government is financed.

Without reform to ensure stable tax revenue, local governments could be weakened to the point of irrelevance. That stable tax revenue must be within the political and legal control of local government institutions. Without such a revenue source, local governments will not be capable of efficiently and effectively providing services. More important, local governments will continue to cede financial and political control to the states. The only revenue source capable of ensuring a strong and vibrant local government is the property tax.[2] This assertion is intentionally provocative because a failure to address the problems associated with local government finance will have serious consequences. Essentially, without significant financial reforms, local governments will play a far-diminished role in public life—a consequence that is contrary to the best interests of both the American federal system and the American public.

This book expands on this belief by using basic, widely accepted theories, none of which is particularly controversial, or even novel. Essentially, from both an economic and political perspective, local governments are a normative good. But local governments require a certain amount of autonomy over their fiscal affairs to carry out their responsibilities. The property tax is the only source of revenue that provides that autonomy. But public and political pressure have eroded the tax's vitality for decades, and the tax no longer dominates local government finance. The problem for American cities, towns, and counties is that there are no viable alternatives to taxing property, at least none that can ensure fiscal and political autonomy. Thus, the property tax must be strengthened and revitalized if local governments are to continue to play an important role in American society.

Localism as a Normative Good

The obvious assumption being made is that it is important—indeed, perhaps imperative—that local governments continue to actively participate in the federalist system. Most Americans would say that local governments have played and should continue to play such a role. The American federal system has created the richest, strongest, freest nation the world has ever known. And local governments have, since the beginning of the Republic, been an integral part of that system. The American experience has been shaped in no small degree by its system of local governments. Americans have many different views on which types of local governments are ideal. Some prefer the metropolis, some the farm community, and others the endless suburbs. As of June 30, 2002, 87,849 local government units were spread across the United States. That number includes 3,034 counties, 19,431 municipalities, 16,506 townships, 13,522 school districts, and 35,356 special districts (U.S. Census Bureau 2002). It makes little difference, at least for purposes of this book, whether one believes that large cities, rural towns, or suburban counties are the ideal vehicle for local governance. What is important is that the American people favor local governance, a fact confirmed by years of public opinion research.

Chapter 2 begins by describing how local governments have served American society. It also sheds light on why local government is so important to American citizens. The logic of localism is grounded in two interrelated virtues that resonate with citizens. Local governments are efficient providers of the most visible, and many of the most important, public services. Moreover, local governments enhance and foster democratic values and civic participation.

That local governments are efficient—that is, they can most closely match public services with citizen demands—is almost beyond dispute. Americans have come to expect certain services—such as police protection, emergency ambulance services, elementary and secondary education, and local roads—that can be provided more effectively and efficiently by local governments than by the federal or state governments. The efficiencies of local government have led to the belief that public services should be provided by the jurisdiction covering the smallest area over which benefits are distributed (for example, see Oates 1972). Americans do not look to their state capitals or federal government to provide fire and police protection, trash removal, or animal control. Rather, Americans look to their mayors, city councils, and county supervisors to perform such services.

In addition to effectively providing fundamental services, local governments serve another important role. They promote democratic ideals and practices, a view held by American political philosophers since the time of Thomas Jefferson. Citizens are much more capable of influencing public policy within their locality than they are at either the state or federal levels of government. Citizens know the policies that they would like to see pursued and can monitor whether these services are being performed in a satisfactory manner.

Local political leaders recognize the visibility of local services and are thus attuned to the wishes of their constituents. This, in turn, reinforces confidence in the public's ability to influence their local government. For this reason, scholars have found that local governments are more responsive than states or the federal government to citizens' demands. This responsiveness is one reason to protect and strengthen the American system of local government.

Localism requires a certain degree of fiscal autonomy; local governments must have some political and legal control over the amount of revenue they can raise and spend. This control must be exercised without undue influence by higher levels of government, particularly at the state level. Without such autonomy, local governments cannot effectively provide the services their residents demand. Without fiscal autonomy, local governments are almost irrelevant in the American federal system of government.

The need for fiscal autonomy is easy to understand. The three levels of government—federal, state, and local—have worked because each level is governed democratically. The elected leaders are accountable to the public. One way that accountability is accomplished is through elected officials providing the public services—be they spaceships or kindergarten teachers—that the citizens demand. To do that, officials raise and lower taxes to pay for those services. If the citizens are not getting the services they want, they will express their displeasure at the ballot box or they will relocate to another city or town. The effectiveness of the system depends on the ability to raise (or lower) taxes in order to provide the necessary level of services at prices citizens are willing to pay.

The threat many localities face is that the fiscal autonomy of local governments has been declining for several decades. Today, local governments have less control over their fiscal affairs than at any time in American history. Local fiscal autonomy is being superseded by state centralization of local finance. State governments are increasingly taking over public services traditionally provided and paid for by localities. By ceding financial control to the states, however, localities cede political control over local affairs. And that is the danger this book seeks to address.

Political and Economic Constraints on Localism

Local governments' ability to raise revenue in a federal system is inherently limited. Chapter 3 describes those limitations in terms of three interrelated political and economic imperatives that generally govern the actions and affect the tax policies of local governments in the United States. The imperatives profoundly affect local tax policy.

First, local governments must provide the basic fundamental services that their residents demand. The streets must be policed, the trash collected, and the children educated. There is little room for debate as to whether local governments must provide these services; they do so a priori.

Second, local governments must promote and protect the wealth of their citizens. Local governments do so by competing with other areas to attract firms and individuals who will contribute more in taxes than they will consume in services, protective zoning practices, and the provision of high-level public services at modest tax costs. Local governments also direct much of their energy toward increasing and maintaining housing values, since the home is the most valuable asset of most citizens.

Third, except in the largest cities, local governments cannot engage in redistributive policies, and they cannot impose progressive taxes. Redistributive policies run counter to the imperative to foster economic wealth. Attempts to redistribute wealth inevitably lead to an out-migration of wealthier residents and an in-migration of poorer residents. This limitation has long been recognized by academics, and more important, by political leaders (Peterson 1981).

Still, it is possible to construct a tax system that comports with the imperatives discussed above while ensuring a meaningful level of local autonomy over fiscal affairs. Chapter 3 also describes the principles of sound tax policy and their application to local public finance. Those principles include fairness, efficiency, accountability, and neutrality. But they are applicable to all governments. Because of local governments' place in the federal system, they must operate under additional guidelines.

Sound local tax policy must be guided by the benefits principle of taxation rather than by one's ability to pay. Benefit taxes are designed to tax only those receiving local public services. Ability-to-pay principles imply progressive or redistributive taxes that cannot function effectively for local governments. In addition, local fiscal policy must be grounded in the taxation of immobile tax bases to the greatest extent possible. Local government efforts to tax mobile bases, such as intangibles or corporate profits, inevitably fail.

The Logic of the Property Tax

Within the framework of sound local tax policy, the property tax is the only viable source of own-source tax revenue for local governments. Since the beginning of the nation, the property tax has dominated local public finance. Chapter 4 explains why the property tax has served the needs of local governments so well for so long.

The property tax has long provided a stable and reliable source of revenue for local governments. Property tax revenue grows as property values increase. Because over time property values have always increased, local government officials can rely on a steady source of increasing revenue without the political costs of raising rates. Because the tax base is immobile, local governments can easily predict revenue yields from year to year. No other source of revenue offers such reliability.

Moreover, administration and compliance with the property tax is relatively easy and thus inexpensive. Once again, this virtue arises because the underlying tax base—the land or improvements thereto—is immobile. For government, the tax base is easily identifiable. While land values change, most local government administrators can easily ascertain the number of acres, parcels, and buildings within the area. Another advantage of the property tax from a governmental perspective is that taxpayers cannot easily hide or move property. Thus, evading the property tax is virtually impossible. The tax presents equally attractive compliance benefits for the taxpayer. Most residential property owners face minimal compliance costs. Unlike for federal and state income taxes, taxpayers do not have to file forms to comply with property tax laws. The government calculates the property tax value and the amount of tax due. The taxpayer's compliance begins and ends with the payment of the tax.

Most important, the property tax has endured because it is conceptually attractive. As opposed to state sales and income taxes, property tax revenue is raised locally to support local public services. Thus, the connection between the source of the revenue, the property, and the services being provided is strong. In this respect, the property tax functions as a benefits tax, precisely the way most public finance experts believe local government should be funded.

A Good Tax under Siege

Although the property tax has dominated local government finance, it has come under intense political pressure. The percentage of total government revenue raised from real property taxes has continuously declined for decades. Local governments once raised more than 80 percent of their own-source tax revenue and 65 percent of total revenue from real property taxes. While collections vary widely by state, the property tax now accounts for less than 40 percent of local government tax revenue and just 25 percent of total revenue.

The reasons for this precipitous decline are explained in chapter 5. The overriding cause of the decline of the property tax has been the public's deep-seated dislike of the tax. For decades, public opinion polls have identified the property tax as the "worst" tax. The public's dislike of the tax arises from the fact that the tax is highly visible; the tax traditionally must be paid in a single lump sum once a year. Citizens also dislike the tax because of past administrative problems; local governments have had difficulties fairly valuing property for tax purposes. Part of the problem of accurately valuing property stems from the fact that property tax burdens continue to increase. In any event, that view has created a strong bias against the tax. Political leaders and the press routinely characterize the property tax as unfair and as the "most hated" tax. These negative sentiments affect people's perception of the tax.

The public's unhappiness with the property tax spurred a series of property tax revolts in the late 1970s and early 1980s. The revolts led to significant limitations on local governments' ability to raise property tax revenue. Today, 44 states restrict property taxation in some way. Limitations apply to rates, assessment increases, and the total amount of revenue that can be collected from the tax. These restrictions have seriously curtailed both revenue collection and the ability to rely more heavily on the tax in the future.

The property tax also has a continuously shrinking tax base. As explained in chapter 5, local governments lose billions of dollars each year from exemptions for charitable organizations and economic development. Nonprofit organizations, including churches, schools, and hospitals, have received property-tax exemptions throughout American history. Local governments, in competing for business investment, also grant property-tax exemptions to firms willing to relocate to their jurisdiction. Property-tax exemptions and targeted tax exemptions have serious consequences for local governments.

Finally, the ongoing debate over school finance has further reduced popular and political support for the property tax. Traditionally, citizens were willing to pay property taxes to support public education (Fischel 2001b). However, local governments' reliance on property taxes to fund public education has created fiscal inequities between property-rich localities and property-poor localities. One remedy to this problem has been the replacement, often under court mandate, of local school property taxes with state funds. Once property taxes no longer primarily fund local education—that is, once the connection between the local public service and the local tax is lost—public support for the tax evaporates.

There Are No Alternatives to Taxing Property

With the property tax under siege, local governments have increasingly turned to other sources of tax revenue to pay for public services. Chapter 6 describes local-option sales and excise taxes. These consumption taxes are the second-largest source of tax revenue for local governments after the property tax.

Local governments impose these taxes in much the same way as states do. In many cases, these taxes are usually collected as part of the state tax. That is, the vendor collects the tax and remits it to the state. The state then returns the local portion of the tax revenue to the jurisdiction in which the purchase was made. The tax offers administrative and compliance conveniences to both the government and the taxpayer. Local governments have minimal responsibilities with respect to administration. Individual taxpayers incur virtually no costs in complying with the tax. Despite lingering concerns over fairness, consumption taxes enjoy widespread support among the public.

Nonetheless, local-option sales and excise taxes are unlikely to play an important role in the future of local government finance for several reasons. First, the overall sales tax base has been steadily falling as more goods and services consumed by Americans are exempt from tax. The continuing shift from an economy based on manufacturing and tangible personal property to one dominated by services and intangible personal property has greatly reduced the tax base. Moreover, political leaders, recognizing the inherent regressivity of the sales tax, have exempted virtually all goods and services deemed necessities. Thus, in most states, food, medicine, and utilities are exempt from tax. The debacle over electronic commerce has also lessened interest in local-option sales taxes. Today, most of what Americans consume is not subject to sales tax. For these reasons, most public finance experts do not believe local-option sales and excise taxes are an adequate or viable source of revenue for local governments. They certainly will not be able to replace the property tax as a source of local revenue.

Local governments also impose local-option income and business taxes as a means of raising revenue. These taxes are discussed in chapter 7. Local governments do not rely on income or business taxes as much as they rely on local-option sales taxes. Only a handful of states allow local governments to tax personal or business income. Local governments have not taxed income more extensively for several reasons. First, local-option income taxes can have a detrimental effect on the local economy. Both the public and the political leadership perceive that local governments are better off without such taxes. This perception feeds the existing bias among state political leaders against income taxes. The local-option income tax is not a viable alternative for local governments and will not move beyond its current status.

Local-option business taxes are even less likely to assume a more important role in financing local government. Because of the mobility of capital, local governments cannot effectively tax business activity, especially in the modern economy, where business is less dependent on land and immobile equipment. Few states now allow local governments to tax businesses, and political leaders have little motive for expanding the reach of local business taxation.

With property taxes under siege and other tax sources limited, local governments have been forced to rely more heavily on nontax revenue. Chapter 8 presents the two most important sources of nontax revenue, intergovernmental aid and user fees and charges. Intergovernmental aid is the largest single source of revenue for local governments. State governments fund local government services, especially elementary and secondary education, more than ever. They are doing so, in part, because local governments' ability to raise adequate amounts of revenue continues to be limited. They are also doing so because of the court-ordered centralization of public education finance. In either event, such aid is damaging to the concept of localism.

State financing of local government gives rise to several problems. First, such financing is inefficient. Relying on political leaders in the state capitals to fund local police, fire protection, ambulances, and schools virtually guarantees that those and other essential local public services will not be adequately funded. State political and policy leaders are too far removed to ascertain local government service needs. This distance erodes the political accountability that helps ensure local government efficiency.

Second, state financing inevitably results in less local political control. All state aid carries rules and regulations for how local governments must spend the money. Governors and legislators have a greater say in how money sent to cities, towns, and counties will be spent. The historical record suggests that all forms of financial centralization are accompanied by such "strings." State control over spending can affect everything from the kinds of books in the local library, to the number of police officers on the street, to the curriculum in the schools, to the artwork adorning local public buildings.

Equally important, increased state funding also creates long-term uncertainties for local government finance. When states face budget crises, the first expenditure they often cut is aid to local governments. During the state budget problems of 2001–02, for example, virtually every state slashed intergovernmental aid.

Moreover, state political leaders are forced to decide among competing interests for government aid. For example, when states run budget surpluses, as they have in recent years, politicians are always under pressure to cut taxes. But the excess revenue may be better spent on local public services. When states run budget deficits, state lawmakers are reluctant to increase taxes to support local public services. The problem is that it is impossible to determine the effects of state financial control of local government. That uncertainty alone should give all Americans pause about the wisdom of ceding financial control over important local public services to the states.

User fees and charges are widely used by local governments—in large part because of the limitations placed on other sources of revenue. Over the past quarter-century—essentially since the onset of the tax revolts— state and local governments have increasingly relied on user fees and charges to fund public services. User fees and charges are among the most, if not the most, efficient methods of financing public services. For that reason, public finance experts regard user fees as an effective means of financing local government (Oates 1993). When the public pays for services directly, the government is less likely to over- or underproduce the service. Local governments can thus better gauge demand for the service, making user fees the ultimate benefit tax.

User fees and charges, however, are incapable of raising enough revenue to meet public service demands, because they have a limited base. For administrative reasons, local governments cannot impose user fees on services widely available to the public. In addition, they cannot, for political reasons, impose fees on many services deemed necessities. Market forces limit the size of fees: Local governments cannot charge more for the underlying service than the public would be willing to pay. And at this point, local governments have imposed user fees and charges on just about everything they can. For these reasons, user fees and charges will continue to play an important, but limited, role in financing local government.

Raising Revenue in the Modern Economy

Local governments face serious limitations on their ability to raise revenue, and the financial constraints are likely to worsen. The rapidly changing economy and the demographic makeup of society will have profound effects on the tax systems of all levels of government, but the effects may be the greatest on American localities. Chapter 9 discusses some of the many challenges that local governments will continue to face.

The continuous shift from manufacturing to a service-based economy will have the greatest impact on local taxation. Business no longer comprises mostly factories with extensive plants and equipment. Manufacturers that sell tangible personal property no longer dominate the economy. Rather, modern American businesses are more likely to use high technology and intangibles to create and sell services. Many modern businesses no longer need extensive real property holdings (which local governments were able to tax), and many no longer exclusively sell tangible personal property (the sales of which are also subject to tax).

International trade has also changed local government finance. Interlocal competition has traditionally placed limits on local government taxation. Cities and towns, once competing with other jurisdictions within a metropolitan area or within a state, are now competing with jurisdictions worldwide. Intergovernmental competition has long placed pressure on local governments vying for business investment, particularly with respect to taxes on mobile bases. Local governments cannot effectively tax mobile capital, as many owners will move the capital out of the jurisdiction. That problem is magnified in a global economy.

Deregulation of key industries, such as electricity, gas, telecommunications, and financial services, has also changed state and local business tax systems (Bonnet 1998). Compared with unregulated businesses, regulated industries have traditionally been subject to higher property and other tax burdens. Moreover, many local governments own and operate utilities that provide services, usually electricity, to their residents. Cities own a majority of electric utilities operating in the United States, and the profits of the operations typically fund general government services. Overall, deregulation will likely reduce utility revenue as well as curb property tax revenue.

Finally, demographic changes will challenge local government tax policy. A rapidly aging population will put particular pressure on the property tax. Traditionally, senior citizens have vigorously opposed property taxation to a greater extent than the rest of the population. Part of that opposition stems from the fact that senior citizens, many living on fixed incomes, face rapidly rising tax burdens as a result of property value inflation. The aging population will likely further pressure the already beleaguered property tax.

Possible Solutions

The underlying assumption of this book is that local governments are a normative good, and that they must have a dependable source of revenue to ensure that they operate efficiently and effectively. If that assumption is correct, then only the property tax can provide that revenue. The property tax in its current state, however, cannot provide the revenue necessary to fund local government. Thus, the tax must be strengthened and revitalized if local governments are to retain some measure of political autonomy.

Chapter 10 sets forth several policy proposals that could lead to a more viable property tax and help ensure that American citizens have the option of governing their affairs locally. The property tax will never be strengthened unless public attitudes change. Citizens need more information about the positive attributes of the property tax. Leaders must show the public the connection between the services paid for by the property tax and the value of their property. More important, political leaders must illustrate to the public that property tax is the only source of revenue that will ensure that they have some control over the public services they demand.

To complement this education effort, the excesses of the property tax revolts must be reversed. Essentially, tax experts must encourage a property tax "counterrevolt." Neither economic nor tax policy justifies the most draconian property tax limitations—those on rates and assessments. Attempting to reverse the excesses of the property tax revolts may appear to be a daunting task.

After all, the limitations remain politically popular, and the property tax remains politically unpopular. Moreover, the tax remains unpopular despite that fact that most of the problems that originally gave rise to the public's unhappiness with the tax have been addressed. Strengthening the property tax is possible if reforms retain safeguards for those on fixed income, such as senior citizens. But those safeguards must be better explained to citizens, who are woefully unaware of many of the policies designed to alleviate property tax burdens. Strengthening the property tax will also likely require governments to reduce other local-option taxes as well as state tax burdens.

State and local governments must also address the significant problem of exempt properties. Exemptions for economic development and charitable organizations cost local governments billions of dollars and shift the burden of paying for public services to other taxpayers. State and local governments must limit the amounts of property eligible for exemption.

Of course, state governments must also address the problem of fiscal inequities in education finance. In many states, the remedy for such inequities has been to shift fiscal responsibility to the states, while at the same time limiting local government taxing powers. Methods of equalizing school spending that do not include reducing local taxing authority must be found.

Finally, policymakers and political leaders should consider fundamental local tax reform with an emphasis on split-rate taxation. Split-rate taxation, a version of Henry George's concept of land value taxation, simply involves taxing the value of land at a higher rate than improvements to that land (buildings and other manmade structures). Virtually every public finance expert has lauded split-rate taxation, because taxing land has no effect on economic decisionmaking. At the same time, reducing the tax on improvements provides an incentive for individuals and companies to develop underused or vacant land.

A split-rate tax system would allow local governments to raise revenue according to the three political imperatives under which they operate and to raise the steady source of revenue necessary to provide basic services. Such a system will allow local governments to provide incentives to create and enhance the wealth of the community. Because the tax on land is neutral—that is, it does not distort market decisions—such a system will not involve redistributing wealth. Moreover, because the land is immobile, such a system provides an ideal base for raising revenue in the 21st century. Chapter 10 explains why split-rate taxation has been called the "magic bullet" that can solve many of the problems of local government finance.

Without significant reforms to the property tax system, local governments will continue to cede financial and political control to the states. As this occurs, a fundamental aspect of American government will cease to play an important role in the federal system. Americans should be wary of such an outcome.

NOTES

1. The premise of the book is based on an article written for *State Tax Notes* entitled "To Preserve Local Government, It's Time to Save the Property Tax" (Brunori 2001d).

2. Property taxes for all purposes herein refer to ad valorem taxes on real property (i.e., land and improvements thereto). Taxes on intangibles and personal property are discussed separately.

2

Local Taxation and American Federalism

The case remains strong . . . for leaving local matters in local hands.
                                                    —Wallace Oates, 1999

Virtually every aspect of American life has been influenced by the ability of people in identifiable geographic areas, including large cities, small towns, rural counties, and the suburbs, to govern themselves. Despite how much local governments have contributed to the success of American society, the writers of the U.S. Constitution did not describe or make provisions for such entities. The U.S. Supreme Court has described local governing bodies as "solely creatures of state government and, as such are properly subservient to state authority" (*Hunter v. City of Pittsburgh*, 207 U.S. 161, 1907). Throughout U.S. history, the federal and state governments were capable, theoretically at least, of providing all public services that are now the responsibility of counties, cities, and towns. Yet Americans have, since the beginning of the Republic, voluntarily organized governments smaller than those at the federal or state levels.

In America, political leaders recognized the value of government "closest to the people" by the time of the Revolution. Thomas Jefferson championed small government, which he saw as the best protector of individual liberty. The third president spoke often about the virtues of the New England town and how it embodied democratic values. In addition, de Tocqueville observed that the pattern of local government reflects America's passion for popular sovereignty (cited in Katz 1999).

More than 200 years later, localities are critical to the governance of America. As Norris (2001, 566) notes, "local government autonomy—or the ability of these governments to exercise their police powers broadly within their territories—is sacrosanct in the United States."

This widely held belief extends well beyond commentators primarily interested in local government. For example, an influential report issued by the National Conference of State Legislatures (1997b) asserts that public service responsibilities should be assigned to the lowest level of government to foster accountability and best meet local citizens' needs.

The widespread acceptance of localism is attributable in part to tradition. The original 13 states organized counties, towns, and relatively large cities. Those local governments provided many basic government services regarding public heath and safety. Local governments have provided essentially the same types of public services ever since. As Stevens (1974) notes, local governments in 1972 were providing the same services that they provided in 1902. Ostrom (1983, 106) concludes that "local autonomy is deeply embedded in our system." The tradition of localism goes much deeper than merely the existence of formal governmental structures. The local tradition reflects not only how Americans view their government, but also how they view society.

For generations, Americans naturally identified with hometowns, local schools, churches, and neighborhoods. To support these institutions, Americans look to local governments to provide education, police and fire protection, and basic transportation infrastructure. Citizens know which services their local governments provide and are in a position to hold local political leaders accountable for delivering those services. Historically, Americans have come to expect certain services from their local governments. When traffic lights are broken, trash is uncollected, or cars vandalized, Americans do not look to Washington or their state capitals to place blame or seek resolution.

Part of the dominance is attributable to strongly held political beliefs in the concept of localism. As Briffault (1990a) observes, localism reflects a philosophical preference for decentralized power to lower levels of government. Local governments represent popular and enduring expressions of how Americans feel about government (Katz 1999). Although some scholars disagree with the view that localism represents a positive concept, many recognize the national ideological commitment to local governance (Cashin 2000).

Americans have traditionally favored local governments more than either the state or federal governments. Years of public opinion polling confirm that Americans generally trust, rely upon, and hold a positive view of local government (see, for example, Conlan 1998). According to a recent national poll, many Americans believe that local governments provide more services for the public's tax dollars than the federal or state governments (Kincaid and Cole 2001).

This public preference for local government helps shape American politics. Every U.S. president from Andrew Jackson to George W. Bush has repeated the mantra that government should be "closer to the people." Both Democratic and Republican leaders routinely praise the efficiency and democracy of local government and call for increased local autonomy (see, for example, Bowman 2002).[1]

The Logic of Localism

The widespread acceptance of localism as a normative good is attributable to the beliefs that local governments can efficiently provide the public services demanded by citizens and that local governments advance democratic values. For these reasons, Thomas (1986, 51) asserts that "the American federal system is wed to local socio-economic and political conditions."

Economic Efficiencies

Local governments provide certain public services more efficiently than other levels of government. Essentially, public services are best provided by the jurisdiction covering the smallest area over which benefits are distributed (Gramlich 1993; Oates 1972). As Bird (1993, 211) asserts, "so long as there are variations in tastes and costs, there are clearly efficiency gains from carrying out public sector activities in as decentralized a fashion as possible."

The federal government is best suited to handling national defense, foreign affairs, and the redistribution of income (see Oates 1999a). State governments are in the best position to provide public higher education, maintain intrastate highways, regulate businesses, and administer the legal system (McKinnon and Nechyba 1997). Local governments are best able to provide local transportation infrastructure, sewage and sanitation, police, fire protection, and elementary and secondary education.[2] As one of the most noted observers of fiscal federalism states, "decentralized levels of government have their raison d'être in the provision of goods and services whose consumption is limited to their own jurisdiction" (Oates 1999a, 1121).

The efficiencies of local government are best understood through the Tiebout hypothesis. In one of the most influential articles written on the subject of local government finance, Tiebout (1956) asserted that local public goods could be provided at efficient levels. According to Tiebout, an individual can choose among multiple jurisdictions, opting to live and work in the community that matches his or her preferences. The individual chooses the community by weighing the costs (tax burdens) and the benefits (public services). Because individuals can choose among multiple jurisdictions, local governments will compete to attract individuals by offering a tax–public service mix to meet public demand. Tiebout described a quasi market for public services. Citizens shop for and purchase (through taxes) services provided by local governments.

According to Tiebout's hypothesis, citizens will "vote with their feet" by moving to a locality that provides a more preferable mix of taxes and services. If individuals or firms believe that they are paying too much in taxes for subpar local public services, they will move, if possible, to another town, city, or county. Other researchers have found support for Tiebout's conclusions (see, for example, Percy, Hawkins, and Maier 1995). Local governments in turn compete for citizens and firms by offering attractive public services and amenities at reasonable tax costs. With a large number of local governments available in the United States, citizens have various choices in which to find their preferred mix. People will self-select into political jurisdictions with policies and services that most closely match their preferences. They will create communities with residents who basically agree on the desired public services and the amount of taxes residents are willing or able to pay. In this market, Tiebout's thinking goes, public services are provided at efficient levels because local governments will not produce more—or less—of what residents demand.

Not everyone agrees with Tiebout's hypothesis (see, for example, Cashin 2000; Shaviro 1993). In asserting his thesis, Tiebout made several assumptions that are impossible to defend. For example, Tiebout assumed that citizens enjoy full mobility. That is, everyone can relocate to another jurisdiction that matches his or her preferences. Tiebout also assumed that citizens have all the information they need regarding the tax burdens and public services in other localities, that wages or income do not affect people's mobility, and that local governments can completely control their mix of taxes and services.[3]

Many of these assumptions are problematic (Shaviro 1993). People do not enjoy full mobility, and many do not recognize how much tax burdens and services offered by local governments differ. Moreover, people do not make location decisions solely on the basis of government services and taxes. Family ties, career opportunities, geographic climate, and other variables influence people's relocation decisions. Local governments also do not have unfettered control over the services they provide or the taxes they can impose.

Still, Tiebout offered a valuable theoretical framework for how local governments operate. Since being introduced, Tiebout's theory has been tested and revised to take into account many of the criticisms. For example, Teske and others (1993) found that competitive markets can be driven by a subset of informed consumers who shop between alternate local governments and produce pressure for competitive outcomes that benefit all consumers. Hamilton (1975) asserted that zoning laws allow localities to limit access to households and firms willing and able to pay for services desired by residents. Buchanan (1971) found that local governments must offer wealthy residents better services to prevent their departure.

Tiebout's general theory explains how people, firms, and local governments behave. Under his hypothesis, mobile citizens move among competing local jurisdictions seeking their preferred mix of taxes and services. In fact, according to one study, every five years, half of all American families change residences at least once (Briffault 1990a). It is likely that Tiebout's reasoning plays a role in how families choose their new neighborhoods.

The proliferation of local government entities in the United States supports Tiebout's analysis. Under Tiebout's thesis, citizens will, if possible, create new local governments if existing governments are unwilling or unable to provide the desired mix of services and taxes. In fact, the number of local governments has grown over time to meet the differing tastes of the American public. In 1942, approximately 24,500 municipalities and special districts existed in the United States. By 2002, that number had grown to 71,293 (U.S. Census Bureau 2002). Again, this phenomenon is consistent with Tiebout's theory.

Finally, under Tiebout's hypothesis, local governments aware of resident mobility and desiring increased tax capacity would compete for individuals and firms. After decades of study and debate, many researchers agree that local governments compete (see, for example, Anderson and Wassmer 2000; Bartik 1991; Kenyon and Kincaid 1991; Park 1997). The motivation for the competition varies from the desire to eliminate blight, to expanding the property tax base, to the creation of jobs. Local governments compete by offering lower taxes and better quality services than other localities.

Studies holding other variables constant have shown that Tiebout's hypothesis is accurate (Percy et al. 1995). As Reschovsky (1993, 123) notes, there is "considerable evidence that tax rates and the quality of public services, especially schools, play a role in determining metropolitan area locational choices of both firms and individuals." Sjoquist (1982) found that the presence of competitive governments kept costs down. Wassmer and Fisher (2000) found that variations in household income within a metropolitan area led to the creation of more school districts and special district governments, a finding consistent with Tiebout's hypothesis. Park (1997) found that counties and cities compete in development policy by matching what other counties and cities do.[4]

Tiebout's theory is the cornerstone for the belief that local governments can efficiently provide public services. But Tiebout's theory on mobilization explains only part of the efficiency of local government. According to Oates (1999a), even in the absence of mobility, local governments would be efficient, because residents are likely to influence local government services in ways besides relocation. For example, residents can directly lobby local policymakers. Citizens can also become involved in the electoral process and support politicians who will provide the mix of services and taxes they desire. Local policymakers, in turn, are likely to listen to local constituencies, which have both electoral power and the ability to migrate (Hirschman 1970).[5]

In the end, while many of Tiebout's assumptions were suspect, the underlying hypothesis has stood the test of time. Citizens will gravitate toward localities that offer desired and affordable public services. And local governments, cognizant of citizen desire, will try to attract people and businesses into their jurisdictions. As economist William Fischel (1995, 284) observes, "American voters prefer a Tiebout world."

In this quasi-market, public services are provided in a much more efficient manner than at higher levels of government. As Oates (1999a, 1122) notes, "on grounds of economic efficiency, a presumption in favor of decentralized provision of public goods with localized effects . . . may seem almost trivially obvious."

Political Virtues

The notion of localism encompasses several political virtues. First, localism reflects the American value of liberty. People should be able to live where they like, and they should be able to govern themselves free of outside interference (Swanstrom 2001). Local governments are best able to provide that environment, consistent with the Madisonian belief that multiple governments deter tyranny of the central government. Multiple governments, because of citizen mobility, also deter tyranny of local governments.

The second political rationale for localism is that it promotes democratic values and practices (Frug 1980). That is, a government that is closer to the people will better reflect citizen desires and encourage citizens to participate in public affairs and the democratic process. Oliver (2000) found that residents of larger communities are much less likely to participate in civic activities. As one prominent political scientist observes, "The bedrock of American local democratic theory is that the role of the local government is to reflect the will of the people and that direct individual participation in local government is the best means of achieving this end" (Wolman 1997, 136). Some research suggests that the public supports local government because such government fosters democratic ideals (Haselhoff 2002).

Citizens will engage in public affairs at the local level because local government decisions have a direct effect on their daily lives. Federal and state governments are responsible for tasks that are often far removed from the average citizen's life. By contrast, citizens rely on local government services every day. The roads and public transportation they use to commute, shop, and play are functions of local government. Police, fire protection, emergency medical care, and education, essential services to the health and welfare of most Americans, are functions of local government. When these services are not adequately provided, the citizens can be expected to voice their disapproval at city council offices, school board meetings, and the ballot box (Bish and Ostrom 1973). Some evidence suggests that citizens are more active in, and successful at, influencing local government than state and federal government (Inman and Rubinfeld 1997).

At the same time, local political leaders are more likely to be respon-sive to the concerns of their individual constituents. The close proxim-ity to the people makes it easier for local officials to ascertain the desires and needs of the public (McKinnon and Nechyba 1997). With fewer constituents, each citizen's voice has a greater chance of being heard. In smaller governmental units, each individual vote counts more. Political leaders and administrators understand this concept and are more likely than state or federal officials to heed the wishes of their constituents. Because local officials are responsive, citizens are empowered to partici-pate in public affairs.

Another political virtue of localism is the fact that decentralized gov-ernments are more apt to experiment with public policies (McKinnon and Nechyba 1997). While discussed much more at the state level, experimen-tation exists at the local government level as well. The underlying theory is that with many local governments free to establish spending and tax policy, experimentation will be more common. Those experiments involve less political risk since they are isolated. The advantage for the federal sys-tem is that successful policies will be mimicked by other governments, while unsuccessful policies will be disregarded.

That local government enhances democratic practices, a view expressed by Thomas Jefferson more than 200 years ago, is a concept that continues to resonate with the American public.[6]

Localism and Taxing Authority

The theory of localism outlined here depends on local governments hav-ing an independent source of revenue within their political control (Peter-son 1995a). That is, local governments, through their elected officials, must have the ability to impose taxes on their citizens without undue interference from state or federal laws. Without such ability, local govern-ments cannot effectively or efficiently provide public services or respond to the needs of their citizens.

More fundamentally, tax autonomy is at the heart of the justification of most systems of elected local government. If local governments lack the ability to set spending priorities and determine tax burdens, the elec-tion of local representatives serves little purpose (Goldsmith 1997).

As Bird (1993, 211) states, "Local governments should not only have access to those revenue sources that they are best equipped to exploit—

such as residential property taxes and user charges for public services—but they should also be both encouraged and permitted to exploit these sources without undue central supervision."

Local governments have never enjoyed unfettered control over their finances. Indeed, their taxing and spending powers have always existed by the grace of state law. Virtually all taxing power arises from state law. Long before Proposition 13, local governments were limited in their ability to raise revenue. State restrictions on local tax authority can be traced back to the mid-19th century. Most states have limited property tax rates and assessments throughout American history. In 1962—nearly 20 years before to the onset of the tax revolts—43 states had some constitutional or statutory limitation on property taxes (Sokolow 1998).

Sales, income, and other taxes have been subject to even more restrictions; those taxes are generally prohibited without statutory approval or constitutional amendment. Historical restrictions, however, have rarely been so onerous as to prevent local governments from providing the basic services their citizens demanded. Local governments have generally enjoyed wide latitude with respect to their public finances.

That wide latitude reflects society's belief that each level of government should be governed democratically. The three levels of American government have worked exceedingly well because each level is governed democratically. The citizens of the United States elect national, state, and local leaders, and those leaders are accountable to the public. One way that accountability works is that elected officials provide the public services—be they spaceships, state universities, or kindergarten teachers—that the citizens demand. To do that, officials raise and lower taxes to pay for those services. If the citizens are not getting the services they want (or if they are getting too many), they will express their displeasure at the ballot box. If the costs of these services go up, local officials and the citizens decide how and whether to pay. Cities and counties can raise taxes. They can curtail services. In many instances, local governments can borrow money. They have flexibility to meet the needs of their citizens. If the local leaders are not meeting their needs, the citizens can choose new leaders.

The linchpin in the local system is local governments' ability to raise and access own-source revenue to provide services (Bird 1993; Bowman, MacManus, and Mikesell 1992; Giertz and McGuire 1991; McGuire 1995; Oates 1991; Sokolow 1998). All three levels of government have traditionally enjoyed access to their own revenue sources. The federal government has primarily used income taxes to fund its operations, states have used a combination of income and consumption taxes, and local governments have relied primarily on property taxes to pay for the services their citizens demand.[7]

Fiscal autonomy requires that local governments have the ability to raise and lower taxes. Accordingly, local government associations regularly request expanded taxing authority from their states, especially when states slash intergovernmental aid during economic downturns. Because localities have traditionally controlled their revenue, they have been the most responsive, accountable, and innovative segments of the federal system.

Even local governments with secure own-source revenue are not always capable of financing the minimum levels of public service. With or without restrictions, many localities have difficulty raising adequate amounts of own-source revenue, particularly in localities with high concentrations of low-income residents, little commercial activity, or declining property values as well as in large cities plagued by declining tax bases and increasing demands for public services.

The inability of some localities to raise adequate revenue often leads to great disparities in ability to raise own-source revenue between local governments even in the same metropolitan region. These disparities usually prevent poorer jurisdictions from providing public services comparable to wealthier localities. These disparities often prevent local governments from providing even minimally acceptable levels of what are considered fundamental public services.

The solution to such fiscal inequities is not to limit local governments' financing authority or to transfer responsibility for providing all local services from the local to state governments. Rather, the states should minimize disparities between rich and poor local governments by intergovernmental transfers. That is, the states should provide monetary aid to poorer communities to help equalize the financial capabilities of rich and poor local governments. Such aid would not come at the expense of localism and local taxing authority.[8] But it would provide the means for poorer communities to achieve some minimum level of financing for such fundamental public services as education, public safety, and transportation.

Despite the problem of fiscal inequities, there is a strong case that local government should be given wide latitude on taxing matters. As Bird (1993, 211) noted, "Unless local governments are given some level of freedom with respect to local revenue . . . the development of responsible and responsive local government will remain an unattainable mirage."

Fiscal Autonomy under Siege

The case for local taxing authority is almost self-evident in the American federalist system. Local political autonomy, a bastion of American government, is dependent on the ability of a locality to raise its own revenue. Yet the trend has been for less local taxing authority and much more centralization of state-local finances. As Sokolow (1998) found, state control over local government finances has been increasing for more than two decades. And the rising state share of state-local revenue best illustrates the increased level of state control. In 1970, the state share of state-local tax revenue averaged 55 percent across the United States. By 2000, that percentage had risen to 61 percent (U.S. Census Bureau 2000).

The loss of local autonomy has occurred by giving statewide voters and legislators control over tax rates and other rules such as assessment and valuation practices. In many states, local tax policy is set through statewide referendum and initiative processes. In many states, the legislature has taken the lead in establishing the parameters of local taxing power. The lost autonomy has occurred partly as a result of state control over services, once the sole responsibility of local governments. The lost autonomy has also occurred as a result of the increased intergovernmental aid from states to localities. As explained in later chapters, intergovernmental aid has by all accounts significantly curtailed local taxing authority (Levine and Posner 1981). Local political leaders have become dependent upon state aid.

As discussed in more detail in subsequent chapters, the tax limitation has also seriously eroded local taxing authority, particularly with respect to property taxes (Shadbegian 1998). The property tax, long the dominant source of revenue for local governments, has been under siege since the tax revolts of the late 20th century. As discussed in more detail in chapter 5, between 1970 and 1995, 43 states adopted 68 different measures limiting the ability of local governments to raise revenue. The overwhelming majority of these laws were aimed at the property tax. Indeed, 34 states imposed limits on property taxes in the wake of Proposition 13 (Brown 2000).

Unlike most of the limitations that existed throughout American history, the tax revolts spurred draconian limitations that often had a crippling effect on local government finance. As Sokolow (2000) found, the property tax restrictions have led directly to diminished local government autonomy and increased fiscal centralization. The various limitations have forced local governments—even those that would otherwise be self-sufficient—to increasingly rely on state aid to fund services once paid for exclusively by the localities.

Conclusion

Americans value local government. There is little doubt that the concept of localism enjoys widespread public and political support. American federalism is presumed to include a strong local government component. And this presumption deserves to be taken seriously. The three levels of American government have served the nation and citizens well. The system has led to the freest, strongest, and richest nation in recorded history. While one may argue over the relative importance of local governments and their appropriate specific roles, the logic of localism cannot be denied. And the inclination should be to protect and strengthen this important aspect of the American federalist system.

There is also no doubt that a strong and vibrant local government system is dependent upon a measure of fiscal autonomy. To provide public services efficiently and foster democratic values, local governments need the ability to raise revenue with minimal interference from higher levels of government. Cities, towns, and counties, through their elected officials, must be able to define tax bases, set rates, and establish tax burdens. As will be discussed throughout this work, however, local tax authority is increasingly under pressure.

NOTES

1. The concept of localism is not limited to the United States. Decentralization and local autonomy are being discussed around the globe. For example, the countries of the former Soviet Union have been establishing local governments and intergovernmental finance systems since the early 1990s (Bird and Wallich 1993). And developing countries have increasingly turned toward decentralized governmental systems as a means of escaping inefficient government (Bahl and Linn 1992).

2. Local governments, particularly those with small populations or in small geographic areas, cannot always provide public services as efficiently as possible. When economies of scale are needed, local governments often voluntarily enter into agreements with other localities to provide public services on a more cost-effective and efficient basis (Swanstrom 2001). Such voluntary arrangements are not inconsistent with the notion of localism.

3. The theory is also criticized for creating the implication that some people "choose" not to live in communities with poor public services (Frug 1999). To be sure, all rational people desire quality services. But like any market, resident choices depend on residents' willingness and ability to pay for those services.

4. In addition to these examples, many studies support Tiebout's theory (see, for example, Grossman, Mavros, and Wassmer 1999; Parks and Ostrom 1981; and Schneider 1986, 1989).

5. Of course, even the "voice" option is not available to all citizens. Many people do not have the information or financial resources to influence policymakers (Gillette 1996).

6. Not everyone views localism as a normative political good, particularly for metropolitan areas (Briffault 1997). That localism inevitably leads to more homogeneous communities has led many scholars to criticize the effects of local autonomy. Frug (1998) argues, for example, that the "privatized conception" of local services has become a major ingredient in fostering the division of localities of privilege and need marked by lines of class, ethnicity, and race.

7. Musgrave (1983) suggests that, ideally, local government should be financed by user fees and property taxes, state governments through consumption taxes, and federal government through income taxes. That "ideal" has largely been accomplished in the United States.

8. That is not to say redistribution of wealth would not occur at all. State subsidies to local governments would presumably come from broad-based taxes on income and consumption. Such taxes would inevitably be disproportionately collected in the wealthier communities and redistributed to the poorer jurisdictions.

3

Local Limits

It is the business of local authority to mend the roads.
—Lord James Bryce, 1921

Mobility of citizens and businesses places political and economic limits on local governments, particularly with respect to tax policy. For example, a citizen desiring better schools can move his or her family to a county with lower taxes and better test scores. Large businesses supplying an area with jobs can threaten to relocate and pressure local politicians into promising them significant tax breaks. These limits on local taxation, which arise as a result of the U.S. federal system, determine which types of services a local government must provide and which types of taxes it will impose to pay for these services. That local governments operate under the constraints described herein is in no way inconsistent with the concept of local autonomy. Indeed, the public's commitment to localism has coexisted with these limitations since the beginning of the nation. Still, the limits profoundly affect local tax policy. This chapter describes the limits the federal system places on local government policy and explains what it takes to build a workable tax system within the parameters of those limits.

The Politics of Taxation

In the United States, taxes play an integral part in political and legislative outcomes at all levels of government (MacManus 1999). Taxes matter both to voters and to business interests; consequently, they matter to politicians. Taxes represent both the opportunity for and restraints upon public service. From a government operations standpoint, taxes determine the level of service the citizens will receive. But they also reflect the cost of paying for those services. Since politics are by definition all about the divisions of power and wealth, taxation is at the core of all governmental decisions. Thus, understanding tax policy requires a "recognition of the political environment within which tax policy is made" (Holcombe 1998, 359).

In the federal government and the state governments, the politics of taxation typically play out in two primary arenas, at the ballot box and before the legislatures. Tax policy arguments aim to influence election outcomes or the enactment of laws. Electoral politics generally center on convincing a majority of voters to support a given candidate. In many elections over the past quarter-century, a candidate's position on taxation has been one of the deciding factors (see, for example, Brunori 2001e; Youngman 1997a).

Legislative politics are more complex. Federal and state politicians use the legislative process to accomplish many goals. They must satisfy the needs and desires of constituents in general and political supporters in particular. In this regard, taxes are often seen as a means of redistributing wealth. But they must also endeavor to make the jurisdiction, whether a state or the nation, economically competitive. Taxpayers usually perceive an area with efficient services and relatively low tax burdens for businesses and individuals, especially for those with political influence, as competitive. Legislative tax politics must address these concerns.

Legislative and electoral tax politics play a similar, if more limited, role in local government. Local candidates often feature tax policy in their campaigns, and they also influence many local elections. Local legislatures (i.e., city and county councils) allocate tax benefits and burdens based to some extent on political influence. For example, one study found that municipal leagues and education associations lobbied for property tax increases, while business groups, taxpayer associations, and farm organizations opposed property tax increases (Bingham, Hawkins, and Hebert 1978). Direct lobbying was the preferred method for all of these organizations.

Tax politics at the local level are unique in several important respects. Unlike the federal—and to a lesser extent, state—government, in the federalist system localities are restrained from using the tax system to redistribute wealth. Thus, political debates on local taxation rarely center on questions of vertical equity or progressivity. Local governments, even in the largest cities, are not significant providers of welfare services.

The overriding tax issue for local governments concerns finding the money to pay for the public services their constituents demand. Roads, schools, police, and other services require cities and counties to raise billions of dollars in revenue every year. Like the political obstacles to raising taxes, the fundamental need to raise revenue to provide services demanded by the public proceeds without respite.

The political challenge for the vast majority of U.S. local governments is that their dependence on the states for their taxing authority limits their ability to raise revenue. All local taxing power emanates from state statutory or constitutional law. State political leaders ultimately control many aspects of local taxation. Thus, local political leaders have limited discretion in the area of tax policy and, consequently, in the area of spending. Many state governments, particularly those in the South, must approve local efforts to adopt new taxes, to expand the tax base, or to raise rates of existing taxes. In most states, only a constitutional amendment can effect changes to the tax structure.

Because of the legal constraints on their taxing authority, local governments form associations to lobby and advocate their positions before the state legislature. Such government-to-government advocacy has become an important part of the politics of local taxation, especially since the tax revolts in the late 1970s, which seriously hampered local government's ability to collect revenue.

For these reasons the dynamics of tax politics are different at the local government level than at the federal or state levels.[1]

Political Imperatives

While state law largely determines local taxing power, the federal system dictates what local governments can and cannot do about services and tax policy. There are policies that local governments, through the elected leaders, must undertake. And there are policies that, except in the most unusual circumstances, they cannot pursue. That the policies—and thus the politics—of local government are constrained by the federal system has long been recognized by political scientists (Banfield 1961; Dahl 1961; Peterson 1981).

And while there is room for considerable disagreement as to their relative degree and importance, three political imperatives for local government leaders have emerged over the course of American history.[2] First, local governments must provide basic public services demanded by their citizens. Second, local governments must promote, create, and preserve the wealth of their residents. The final imperative is, in fact, a prohibition. Local governments must meet the first two imperatives without pursuing redistributive policies. That is, they cannot redistribute wealth, at least to a meaningful degree, from rich to poor citizens.

Service Provision

Local governments must provide basic public services to their residents. Yates (1984) described local governments as "service delivery systems that provide daily and locality specific public goods to citizens." Basic public services are those that all citizens expect and need to carry on their everyday lives. They include police and fire protection, road repair, emergency health care services, and public education. Peterson (1981) called these basic services "allocative" and theorized that they are provided by government a priori. Bird (1993) notes the main task of local government is to give its constituents what they want and are willing to pay for.

The imperative to provide services at an acceptable level arises in part because local governments are the most efficient and effective at providing certain services. As discussed in chapter 2, local governments are best able to provide the services that benefit citizens in a defined geographic area. But the imperative also arises because Americans have come to expect certain services to be provided by their local governments. That expectation in return arises because local governments have long provided those services. It is ingrained in the American culture that local governments will police the streets, educate children, and provide other fundamental services. If citizens do not receive the services they believe they are paying for, they will, if possible, move to a locality that does provide the services. This fact is not lost on local or state officials (National League of Cities 1998).

There is no doubt that local governments have been primarily and, historically at least, solely responsible for these services. Moreover, the basic services must be provided despite legal, economic, and political challenges that may affect local governments' ability to raise the money to pay for such services. After all, that Commerce Clause restrictions, state mandates, or federal laws may limit local tax options is of little solace to the citizen whose trash is not being collected. When basic public services are not consistently or adequately provided, citizens and businesses eventually either leave or decide not to locate in a particular jurisdiction. When basic government services are not provided to the satisfaction of the public, government leaders also often incur the wrath of the voters, a fact not lost on local politicians.

The importance of these basic services to citizens must not be understated. Transportation, public safety, and education are not luxuries for most citizens, but rather represent the necessities of modern life. For example, that quality of schools is of immense importance to homebuyers has been long known to political leaders and real estate agents alike (Strauss 2001). Public services must be provided in a satisfactory fashion or residents and businesses will take some action, whether that is voicing their concerns or relocating to a city or county that will meet their demands (see Nechyba and Strauss 1998). This is of course consistent with Tiebout's view of how people, firms, and local governments operate.

To be sure, there have been highly publicized examples of local governments failing to provide adequate levels of public services to their constituents, particularly in large cities (Peterson 1994).[3] At different times, New York City, Newark, Cleveland, and Washington, D.C., have been plagued by the inability to collect trash, fix roads, and police the streets. Moreover, in several instances, state governments have taken over local public school systems that have failed to deliver adequate services.

These failures were attributable to severe financial crisis, often caused by economic recession or a rapidly declining tax base. The failure to provide services at acceptable levels was also attributable, at times, to mismanagement. In cases of local governments' failure to adequately provide basic services, many citizens chose to show their dissatisfaction by leaving the local jurisdiction. Those who remained set about the task of electing new leaders who promised to deliver services effectively and efficiently. And despite these periodic failures, the history of local government in America shows remarkable success in providing the services that the public demands.

Local governments must pay for public services. And the ability to raise revenue through taxes is directly related to the level and quantity of these services. Thus, the imperative to provide basic public services runs parallel to the need to collect revenue. This connection is best illustrated by the annual survey of city fiscal conditions commissioned by the National League of Cities (see, for example, Pagano 2002).

Local taxation allows policymakers to raise the requisite revenue to provide the desired level of services. Other sources of nontax revenue (i.e., intergovernmental aid, user fees, and debt) do not offer the reliability or flexibility necessary to provide a consistent service level. In this regard, local government's discretion to set policies—to provide the quality and quantity of services demanded by its citizens—is a function of its ability to impose taxes.

The imperative to provide services prompts local officials to find revenue. Officials would prefer to raise revenue from sources directly in their control. But the need to provide services is stronger than the desire to raise own-source taxes. If the tax revenue necessary to provide the services is not available, local public officials will look to nontax revenue.

Wealth Creation

The second political imperative is that local governments must promote and protect the wealth of the community. Local governments must pursue policies that will enrich their residents, be they individuals or business entities. That local governments operate in an environment that requires a dedication to development policies is a view widely accepted by local government scholars (Dahl 1961; Molotch 1976; Peterson 1981; Swanstrom 1985).[4] Local governments must pursue wealth-building policies, if necessary, at the expense of neighboring jurisdictions. Local governments must undertake such policies because their citizens demand and expect them and because other localities are undertaking them.

Traditionally, fostering economic development has been viewed as encouraging new business creation, more employment, and investment in plants and equipment. As Thomas (1986, 32) notes, the "city's leadership is motivated by a chamber of commerce attitude that growth and development is the city's lifeblood." The academic and professional literature provides illustrations of policies designed specifically to encourage such behavior (see, for example, Kenyon and Kincaid 1991). The incentive to encourage business development arises from the desire to increase a jurisdiction's overall tax capacity. Business investment that leads to additional tax revenue can lower the effective tax burdens on residents.

Local government development policies often include lowering tax burdens, particularly for business interests; easing regulation of commercial activities; and financing infrastructure for new development. Peterson (1981) asserts that such development policies are not a matter of debate, theorizing that development must be local government's paramount task, because it alone advances the city's vital economic interests.[5]

The support for development policies is evident in virtually every segment of society, not just among political and business elites. For example, a 2002 *Washington Post* poll found strong public support for business development policies in poor and minority neighborhoods throughout the nation's capital (Wilgoren 2002). Such findings are consistent with Peterson's view that development policies engender little opposition.

The political imperative to create wealth is usually thought of as requiring strong business development policies. For political leaders, business development is motivated by one goal—increasing tax capacity. Tax capacity can be increased in a number of ways through business development. Increased employment, property values, and commercial activity will, depending on the particular local tax structure, lead to more tax revenue. Studies have shown that such policies generally result in more tax capacity and more public revenue. For example, Oakland and Testa (1995) found that public revenue generated from business development exceeds the costs of public services businesses require.

Fostering economic wealth and development does not necessarily mean building or expanding commercial enterprises. For most individuals, their most valuable asset is their home. Homeowners are intent on maximizing their wealth (Brueckner 1983; Fischel 2001a). Because their major asset is their home, citizens are primarily concerned with maintaining high property values.

Therefore, one important policy objective of local government is to increase real estate values. Such policies might entail improving services that will directly increase values. Such policies involve the use of zoning laws that prevent people or firms that might lower property values from taking up residence. The goal of increasing and maintaining wealth is pursued even when additional commercial development is not possible. Many communities (e.g., those in the suburbs) cannot undertake large-scale business development because they have little land available. Local governments must still protect and enhance the wealth of residents, especially with respect to property values. For many local governments, particularly those in the suburbs, the imperative to increase wealth leads local officials to make increasing home values a priority.

Political leaders often view fostering economic wealth as a goal requiring policies that minimize tax burdens on homeowners (Goldsmith 1997). Such policies may entail zoning measures designed to (1) keep low-income individuals from moving in; (2) preserve open space, at the expense of commercial development, if such preservation increases the property values of neighboring residents; and (3) oppose heavy industry, if such industry will lead to increased pollution. For example, Fischel (1979) found that affluent communities often deliberately oppose industrial development that would increase the local government tax base. In many suburban communities, residents would be willing to forgo additional tax capacity in return for less pollution and traffic congestion. The promotion of wealth takes several forms and is one of the most important goals of local governments.

Avoiding Redistribution

The last political imperative is that local governments must avoid redistributing wealth through either revenue or expenditure policy. Except for a few instances, local governments' attempts to redistribute money from wealthy to poor residents have failed.

Consistent with the belief that only higher levels of government can effectively redistribute wealth, local governments generally refrain from such policies (Peterson 1981). Indeed, local governments cannot effectively undertake policies designed to assist poorer citizens at the expense of wealthier citizens. The imperative against redistribution is consistent with the benefits view of taxation. As Rubin (1998, 29) notes in discussing the tax revolts, "Over time, the model has changed from the rich property owners [sic] unwillingness to pay for services to the poor, to all taxpayers [sic] unwillingness to pay for services and programs from which they do not benefit."

Some local governments, particularly for large cities, provide services such as day care and senior citizen assistance that disproportionately benefit lower-income citizens. Large cities, because of both their size, which can make it difficult to relocate, and their concentrated wealth, are usually in a better position to supply some redistributive services. But local governments cannot undertake meaningful redistribution efforts, such as providing welfare and imposing progressive taxes. For example, one study found that between 1972 and 1989, counties increased expenditures for every program except those designed to redistribute wealth (Park 1996).

As Peterson (1995b) notes, "Any locality making a serious attempt to tax the rich and give to the poor will attract more poor citizens and drive away the rich. No amount of determination on the part of local political leaders can make redistribution efforts succeed. If no other force is able to stop their efforts, bankruptcy will."

Once again it is the federal system that dictates the limitation on redistributive policies. Local governments' attempts to redistribute wealth will attract poorer residents into their jurisdictions. For this reason, attempts at local redistribution of wealth have been short-lived. Peterson and Rom (1989) found, for example, that states that increased welfare benefits experienced an increase in the poverty-level population. The results could be expected to be even more dramatic at the local level, since costs of moving locally are generally lower than moving across state lines. At the same time, wealthier individuals—whose wealth is being distributed—will migrate out of the jurisdiction. Such a scenario is untenable to most politicians and runs counter to the most basic understanding of how local governments operate.

Political Biases

The imperatives described in this chapter have led to two profound political biases: harmful tax competition and exportation of taxes to other areas.

Harmful Tax Competition

As noted in chapter 2, local governments compete for firms and individuals that will enrich the jurisdiction (see Bartik 1991; Kenyon and Kincaid 1991). The imperative to create and preserve wealth inevitably leads to competition among local governments. This competition, especially between metropolitan areas, is an inherent feature of the nation's federal system of government. The permeability of metropolitan government boundaries and the relative autonomy of local decisionmaking create an incentive for local governments to attract and keep taxpayers who contribute more tax revenue than they consume in government services.

How local governments compete for economic development varies. Many governments attempt to offer superior public services as a means of enticing businesses and households. Working infrastructure, low crime, and good schools all make a jurisdiction more attractive to both business and residential interests. Such competition generally enhances the efficiency of government (Duncan 1992). The imperatives to provide public services and promote economic development are closely related.

Local governments also use tax policy to attract businesses, jobs, and residents. Some governments set their overall tax burdens at levels that are competitive with their neighbors' levels. Many local governments form enterprise zones, in which businesses investing in particular areas of a municipality or county receive tax breaks. Enterprise zones enrich low-income areas of the jurisdiction.

In many areas, local governments target tax incentives to specific businesses. Such incentives aim to encourage companies to locate or remain in the jurisdiction. Metropolitan governments are especially inclined to use tax policy to compete, because the other variables that influence location decisions (transportation and labor costs) are often roughly equal across the metropolitan area. While competition is inevitable, many public finance experts view targeted tax incentives as inefficient, inequitable, and largely unnecessary (see, for example, Brunori 1997; Duncan 1992).

Wolman (1988) explains the political logic of incentives, which are rational even if they have a small chance of producing the desired results. The potential benefits of claiming credit for creating jobs and investment significantly outweigh virtually all other considerations. The philosophical debates over the "race to the bottom" or about zero-sum destructive competition have little or no effect on the imperative that local governments compete.

Exporting the Tax Base

A political bias that arises out of the political imperatives described here is the desire to export tax burdens to nonresident individuals and businesses. The bias to export tax burdens occurs not just at the local level but at all levels of government. Political leaders prefer to meet constituent service demands without incurring the risk of placing the burden of paying for those services on those constituents (Hansen 1983). The corollary to the political bias toward tax exporting is that "the public's readiness to demand and consume government programs is . . . greater than its willingness to pay for them" (Citrin 1979, 113).

The propensity to export taxes is particularly notable at the local level, where politicians have numerous ways of exporting tax burdens to residents of other jurisdictions. Some taxes are particularly well suited to be exported to nonresidents. Meals, lodging, and other excise taxes are often imposed because nonresidents purchase a disproportionate amount of the underlying goods or services subject to tax.

But local governments can export burdens through virtually all of their available taxes. For example, property taxes on commercial or industrial property can be shifted to consumers and owners of capital who may or may not live within the jurisdiction. According to one estimate, for every dollar raised from commercial property taxes, 52 cents comes from nonresidents (Pagano and Forgette 2001). Local-option sales taxes can be shifted to nonresidents, particularly to nonresidents who do not reside in localities with heavy commercial development. According to Ladd and Yinger (1989), for every sales tax dollar collected from residents, another 21 cents is collected from nonresidents. Local-option income taxes can also be exported, principally to commuters. According to Pagano and Forgette (2001), for every income tax dollar raised from residents, nonresidents pay an additional $1.27.

Nonresidents should be required to pay some of the costs of the public services they consume. Commuters, tourists, and remote vendors often enjoy public amenities and consume services provided by local governments. The problem, from a tax policy standpoint, arises when local governments attempt to raise more revenue from nonresidents than the costs of providing services to them require.

Tax exporting creates what many economists call a "fiscal illusion." When an area exports its tax burdens, citizens will demand more public services than they would be willing to pay for through their taxes. This mismatch results in an oversupply of public services. For this reason, exporting taxes often creates inefficiency (Bird 1993).

Raising Revenue in an Era of Antitaxation

The inherent structural limitations and the political biases that influence local tax policy are only part of the story. In addition, for much of the past three decades, antitax sentiment has largely shaped the U.S. political landscape. Since the mid-1970s, candidates in both parties and at all levels of government have often campaigned against government in general, and against taxes in particular. Politicians view the issue of taxation with trepidation.

Presidential and congressional politics over the course of the past quarter-century illustrate the importance of tax policy to political success. In the 1970s, Jimmy Carter made tax reform an important part of his platform. In the 1980s, Americans elected Ronald Reagan in part because of his promise to significantly cut federal taxes. George H. W. Bush, for his part, felt the need to make his infamous promise—"no new taxes"—in 1988. Republicans gained control of the U.S. Senate in 1982 and both Houses of Congress in 1994 in part because of their antitax platform. Bill Clinton, to some extent, based his campaign on middle-class and low-income tax cuts. Most recently, George W. Bush made his pledge to cut more than $1 trillion in taxes the centerpiece of his presidential campaign.

The politics of antitaxation are also evident at the state and local levels of government. The last quarter of the 20th century is replete with examples of both gubernatorial and legislative candidates pledging to cut, or at least not to raise, taxes (Brunori 2001e). Even candidates calling for expanded public services typically avoid discussing how such services would be financed. In elections where candidates emphasize tax policy, the side advocating reduced tax burdens generally prevails.

Although politics have often shaped tax policy, it was the tax revolts of the late 1970s and 1980s that had a critical effect on local government finances. Beginning with California's Proposition 13 in 1978, state governments began seriously limiting local governments' ability to rely on property taxes to raise revenue. Within six months of the passage of Proposition 13, tax limitation measures were on the ballots in 17 states, and the measures were approved in all but five states. Forty-three states adopted some form of property tax limitations or relief between 1978 and 1980. By 1994, all but four states (Maine, New Hampshire, South Carolina, and Vermont) had passed laws restricting state and or local government tax or spending abilities (Sexton and Sheffrin 1995).

Much of the cause of the tax revolts is attributable to real and perceived problems with the property tax. Rapid inflation of housing values gave rise to dramatic increases in property tax burdens. This rise had a particularly harsh effect on low- and fixed-income homeowners. The public's lingering unhappiness with property tax administration also fueled antitax sentiments. But deeper political causes were also at work. The recession and political scandals of the 1970s evoked much hostility toward government. Taxpayers were dissatisfied with their tax burdens at all levels of government, and citizens had a sense of frustration toward the federal government. But in many states citizens had an outlet for those frustrations—the initiative process. The availability of direct democracy allowed disgruntled citizens to take on unresponsive politicians and play an active role in the policymaking process. The antitax political environment was strengthened by direct democracy. Indeed, states that allowed initiatives experienced a far higher rate of tax limitation adoptions (Matsusaka 1998).

The primary result of the tax revolts was to debilitate local governments. The tax limitations had a negative influence on local government size and growth (Brown 2000; Shadbegian 1998). They also had serious consequences for many public services, particularly education. Downes and Figlio (1999) confirmed that the imposition of tax and expenditure limits resulted in long-run reductions in public services.

The tax limitation movement has also hampered local governments' ability to provide the basic services that their constituents demand. While the limitations are in place, the local political leaders must still provide services—only with fewer revenue options. This situation has led some politicians to manipulate their services in an attempt to entice voters to override the limitations. For example, some political leaders cut teacher pay by large amounts but reduced administrative costs by small amounts, exaggerating the effect of the limitations on teacher pay (Figlio and O'Sullivan 2001).

Building a Sound Local Tax System

Local government leaders are torn between seemingly irreconcilable pressures. They must provide services and foster economic wealth despite, at times, severe political and legal limitations on raising revenue.

Still, it is possible within this paradox to discuss principles of local tax policy. In general, the question of what constitutes a sound tax has been discussed by public finance experts since the time of Adam Smith. Over the centuries, economists, public finance theorists, and political philosophers have developed a set of criteria by which to evaluate tax systems. These criteria are widely accepted principles thought necessary to raise revenue in a democratic society. Essentially, taxes should (1) provide appropriate revenues; (2) have as little effect on economic activity as possible; (3) be fair and equitable; (4) be easy and economical to administer; and (5) be accountable (see Blough 1955; Reese 1980; Shoup 1937; see also Brunori 2001e for a detailed description of these principles).

While these principles are thought applicable to federal and state revenue systems, local tax policy design must take into account the additional problems posed by the mobility inherent in the local government system.

First and foremost, local governments generally cannot effectively, and therefore should not attempt to, impose progressive taxes. Progressive taxes tend to be most fair when imposed by federal and state governments (Brunori 2001e). As explained above, the imposition of progressive taxes by local governments will drive wealthier residents and businesses out of the jurisdiction. This prohibition poses few problems for local governments. Progressive tax burdens can be attained through personal and corporate income taxes as well as through certain business taxes. But, as will be explained in the chapters that follow, local governments refrain from using such taxes. Wage and payroll taxes are levied in several states, but they have a regressive effect.

Rather than imposing progressive taxes, local tax policy should be guided by the benefits principle. The benefits principle calls for people to pay taxes in proportion to the benefits they receive from government programs. Thus, residents who receive more benefits incur greater tax burdens. Tiebout's hypothesis is not only consistent with this principle, but local government efficiency is dependent upon benefit taxes (Goodspeed 1998). Although taxes, by definition, are not voluntary, taxpayers pay for the services they receive, and the government will provide only those services for which taxes will be paid. Taxes, at least with respect to efficient local government operations, are thus analogous to prices.

Moreover, under the benefits principle, citizens are exposed to the true cost of government. Citizens can better evaluate the extent of government services they desire by their costs. As noted earlier, when citizens are not aware of the tax costs (for example, as a result of exporting), they demand more government services. Operating under the benefits principle reduces such inefficiencies. It is not surprising that many local public finance economists endorse the benefits principle of taxation with respect to local government fiscal affairs (see, for example, Bird 1993; Gramlich 1993; Oates 1993). Indeed, failure to use benefit taxes tends to lead to destructive tax competition (Goodspeed 1998).

Within the framework of the benefits principle, Bird (1993, 214) has outlined seven characteristics of a sound local tax system:

1. The tax base should be immobile to allow local authorities some leeway in varying rates without the tax base disappearing.
2. The tax yield should be adequate to meet local needs and remain sufficiently buoyant (i.e., expand at least as fast as expenditures).
3. The tax yield should be stable and predictable over time.
4. The tax should be perceived as reasonably fair by taxpayers.
5. The tax should be easy to administer efficiently and effectively.
6. It should not be possible to export much, if any, of the tax burden to nonresidents.
7. The tax base should be visible to ensure accountability.

These characteristics are generally consistent with the long-standing principles of sound taxation. The primary differences, taking into account mobility, are the requirements that the tax base be immobile and that it be impossible to export tax burdens to nonresidents. Local attempts to tax mobile bases, such as intangible property or wages, can lead to the out-migration of people and firms. The question of exportability is more difficult to answer. As noted earlier, politicians have a strong political bias toward exporting tax burdens. Yet many economists agree that exporting taxes to other regions is inefficient.

According to public finance experts, the local-option income tax (as opposed to a wage or payroll tax) (Bird 1993), the tax on real property (Oates 1993), and user fees and charges (Gramlich 1993) all generally meet the characteristics outlined here.

NOTES

1. For an in-depth discussion of federal tax politics, see Reese (1980) and Steuerle (1991). For a discussion of state tax politics, see Brunori (2001e), Hansen (1983), and MacManus (1999).

2. The following section borrows heavily from Peterson's *City Limits* (1981). In perhaps the most influential work concerning local government theory, Peterson asserted that development policy was the paramount task for city government.

3. Smaller cities and towns occasionally experience financial and management problems and are unable to meet their service obligations as well (Monkkonen 1995).

4. Scholars vary, often widely, in their assessment of how local governments pursue development policies. But there is widespread agreement that the policies are pursued.

5. Some scholars, such as Stone and Sanders (1987), disagree with the view that development policy is such an imperative that political conflict is not present. Many local government scholars believe that development policies result in conflict, but it is conflict over who will most benefit from the policies (DeLeon 1992; Elkin 1987; Stone 1989). Questions of political conflict aside, local governments must and do undertake policies designed principally to increase and maintain the wealth of their residents.

4

The Logic of the Property Tax

The property tax is an unpopular, often poorly administered, tax which has survived because it makes it possible for the American system of local government to survive.
—Glenn W. Fischer, 1989

The property tax has been the most important source of local government revenue throughout American history (Ladd 1998). Local governments have raised an overwhelming share of their own-source tax revenue from property taxes. The dominance of the property tax has, in no small measure, shaped the history of local governance in the United States. It is not an exaggeration to say that the way local governments operate today has much to do with their traditional reliance on taxing property. That, in turn, raises the question of whether the future of localism is tied intrinsically to the ability to tax property.

This chapter discusses the importance of the property tax and why it has remained a dominant source of revenue for local governments.

Property Taxation in the United States

The property tax is the only tax levied in all 50 states and the District of Columbia. Traditionally, the tax has been the primary source of tax revenue for local governments. While reliance on the tax has steadily decreased, the property tax dominated local government finance

45

throughout the 20th century (Wallis 2001). In 1957, local governments raised more than $12 billion, or 85 percent of their total tax revenue, from property taxes. In 1999, local governments in the United States raised more than $228 billion, or 72 percent of their own-source tax revenue, from property taxes (U.S. Census Bureau 2000). The fact that local governments continue to raise a large percentage of their own-source revenue from property taxes is a testament to the strength of the tax. As discussed in chapter 5, by 1999, public opinion had limited the ability of local governments to use property taxes to fund public services.

The property tax is imposed by counties in 45 states, municipalities in 49 states, townships in 24 states, school districts in 42 states, and special districts in 20 states (Rafool 2002). Not surprisingly, the reliance on the property tax varies by type of local government. Historically, of all types of local governments, large U.S. cities have relied on property taxes the least. This lesser reliance has become even more pronounced since the property tax revolts of the late 1970s. Large cities, because of their geographic size and intense commercial activity, have many more opportunities to raise revenue from other sources, such as levies on sales and income.

With respect to own-source revenues, independent school districts have relied most heavily on property taxes. In 1997, independent school districts raised more than $92.7 billion, or about 98 percent of their total tax revenue and about 80 percent of their total own-source revenue, from property taxes (U.S. Census Bureau 1998). Approximately 43 percent of all residential property taxes in the United States are collected by independent school districts.

With respect to total revenue, townships actually rely most heavily on the property tax. In 1997, townships raised approximately $14 billion, or 56.9 percent of their total revenue, from property taxes (U.S. Census Bureau 1998). Unlike independent school districts, townships do not receive most of their income in the form of intergovernmental aid. The lack of support from state government, and the scarcity of viable alternative sources of revenue, have resulted in townships relying more heavily on the property tax.

Smaller cities and counties have relied more on the property tax than have large cities, but they depend on it less than independent school districts. Unfortunately, few data are available on the use of the property tax by smaller cities. But U.S. Census data show that in 1997, all municipalities in the United States raised $45.9 billion, or about 15 percent of their total revenue, from property taxes. Municipalities raised about 28 percent of their total tax revenue from property taxes in 1997. At the same time, American counties raised approximately $47 billion, or 22 percent of their total revenue, from property taxes. Although revenue from property taxes accounts for a relatively small percentage of total revenue, about 70 percent of counties' total tax revenue comes from property taxes.

Special districts also raise the bulk of their tax revenue from property taxes. In 1997, special districts raised about $8 billion, or 80 percent of their tax revenue, from property taxes (U.S. Census Bureau 1998). Special districts, however, rely much more heavily on user fees and charges than other types of government do. Accordingly, property taxes accounted for only 8 percent of total special district revenue.

Property tax reliance also varies, often greatly, by region. U.S. local governments in the Northeast and Midwest have traditionally relied more heavily on property taxes than have local governments in the South or in the West (Minnesota Taxpayers Association 2001). In 1999, for example, New Hampshire, Maine, Vermont, New Jersey, Rhode Island, and Connecticut collected the most in property taxes as a percentage of personal income. Conversely, Alabama, New Mexico, Oklahoma, Hawaii, Kentucky, West Virginia, and North Carolina collected the least (Hill 2002). Not coincidentally, regions in the nation that rely most heavily on property taxes have also had the strongest commitment to local autonomy; a clear connection between the property taxes and local autonomy exists.

Differences within regions are also evident. New Jersey, for example, is considered a high-property-tax state. In 2000, local governments in New Jersey raised $14 billion in property taxes, more than the revenue collected from the state's three largest taxes combined. The property tax accounted for 47 percent of all of New Jersey's state and local tax revenue in 2000— far above the national average of 30 percent. Moreover, New Jersey collected 98 percent of all its local own-source tax revenue (excluding user fees) from property taxes, compared with 75 percent nationwide. By contrast, in neighboring New York, the property tax accounted for 61 percent of all local own-source revenue (excluding fees), an amount well below the national average (Coleman, Hughes, and Kehler 2001).

Similarly, in Alabama, traditionally a low-property-tax state, local governments raised a mere 37.9 percent of their total 1999 revenue from property taxes. But local governments in its border state, Mississippi, raised 91.8 percent of their total revenue from property taxes, more than most other states (Rafool 2002).

Virtues of the Property Tax

The property tax remains an important source of revenue for local governments essentially because it meets all the characteristics of a sound local tax system outlined in chapter 3 (Bird 1993). As explained in detail in chapter 5, the property tax has been intensely criticized for decades. It is the one of the most politically unpopular taxes. Yet it continues to generate significant revenue for local governments.

The virtues of the tax that have given rise to its importance are well documented and have been recognized by public finance scholars throughout the 20th century. The tax has been praised by the intellectual leaders in the public finance field as an ideal source of revenue for local governments (see, for example, Bahl 2001; Bird 1993; Break 1993; Gramlich 1993; Harris 1974; McGuire 2001; Mikesell 1993; Musgrave 1983; Netzer 1966; Oates 1999b; Strauss 2001; Youngman 1998a). The research of leading scholars has led many public finance professionals to endorse the property tax. For example, according to a study conducted in the mid-1990s, 93 percent of the membership of the National Tax Association favored the use of property taxes to fund local government operations (Slemrod 1995).

What Makes the Property Tax So Widely Accepted among Tax Experts?

AN OLD TAX

The well-worn adage "an old tax is a good tax" applies to taxes on property. The property tax remains an important source of revenue for local governments in large part because it has a well-established place in the tax system. This stability supports the argument that society's long-term reliance on the property tax is a normative good. According to the principles of good tax policy, a tax system (particularly the underlying base) should change infrequently (National Conference of State Legislatures [NCSL] 1992). Making changes to a tax system, even in small increments, creates administrative and compliance costs. More important, significant changes disrupt expectations as to what is, and what is not, taxable.

For more than 200 years, local governments have relied to some extent on the property tax to fund public services. The earliest documented U.S. property tax was levied nearly 130 years before the Declaration of Independence (Fisher 1996).

The historical dominance of the property tax is attributable in part to the fact that local governments, for much of America's existence, did not play as extensive a role in providing public services as they do today. While local governments provided basic public safety and transportation services, they did so on a much smaller scale. Public education did not become a widespread local government function until the late 19th century. Put simply, local governments did not spend as much money in 1850 as they did in 1950. Thus, the property tax proved more than adequate to fund the limited local government services offered throughout the early period of American history.

Moreover, the historical dominance of the tax also is attributable to the fact that local governments had few financing alternatives. General sales taxes did not exist in the United States until the Great Depression. At that time, sales taxes were initially levied only at the state level. Federal and state governments had instituted income taxes nearly a generation before that. At the time of their inception, however, government leaders never discussed or debated whether they should impose taxes on local government income. Federal and state governments administered excise taxes. At the time, local political leaders could not even imagine user fees and user charges.

At the start of the 21st century, virtually all American property owners viewed the property tax as a fact of life. Americans may not, indeed by all accounts do not, like property tax. But they have come to accept it as the way local government is financed. Certainly, few property owners are surprised when the property tax bill arrives—because it always arrives.

A STABLE TAX
The property tax has long provided a stable and reliable source of revenue for local governments (Mikesell 1993, 34; Shuford and Young 2000). Stability and reliability are considered two requirements for creating a sound tax system (Blough 1955; NCSL 1997b). Few taxes are more reliable than those on real property. Unlike all other local taxes, the property tax base cannot be moved. The revenue from such a "captive" tax base can be relied on to a greater extent than either wage or sales taxes—both of which have highly mobile tax bases. Local officials can budget for public services knowing that the underlying base will be available to support those services. Moreover, property values change only marginally from year to year and do not respond to economic shifts as rapidly as sales or income taxes (Pagano 2002).

Another principle of sound taxation is that a tax system must not only provide for current spending, but also meet the future revenue needs of the local jurisdiction (NCSL 1992). Property tax revenue has consistently grown over the years. Even from 1980 to 1997, a period during which significant limitations were placed on property tax rates and assessed values, property tax revenue grew dramatically in real terms. Property tax revenue growth has much to do with the fact that real property values appreciate over time. And because real property appreciates over time, property tax revenues continuously grow. Thus, the property tax is uniquely positioned to meet future public service needs.

Equally important from a political perspective, property tax revenue grows without the risks associated with raising rates. Political leaders, while often decrying the property tax, keep the tax in place. Property tax rates are rarely raised to meet the public service demands of citizens. Indeed, property tax revenue often grows faster than the public service demands of local citizens. This phenomenon is not necessarily an unqualified normative good.[1]

The steady growth of property tax revenue and the immobility of the tax base give local governments more flexibility with respect to their fiscal systems. As revenue grows, local officials have the ability to adjust the level of services and tax burdens according to the desires of their constituents. Thus, the property tax is the principal source of fiscal flexibility for local governments (Sokolow 1998).

That flexibility enhances local taxing authority, which in turn strengthens local government political autonomy. That flexibility also affects the efficiency of local governments, as described in chapter 2. The ability to adjust services and burdens to match the demands of the public is dependent on a flexible source of tax revenue. The property tax has provided that flexibility and has arguably enhanced the ability of local governments to operate in an efficient manner.

AN EASY-TO-ADMINISTER TAX

Although not problem-free,[2] local governments' administration of and taxpayers' compliance with the property tax are relatively straightforward and thus inexpensive (Sheffrin 1999). The tax is easy to administer and enforce largely because the underlying tax base—that is, the land and any improvements made to the land—is immobile. For government, the tax base is easily identifiable. Although property values change, local administrators can easily ascertain the number of acres, parcels, and buildings that need to be taxed. Taxpayers cannot easily hide or move property. Thus, unlike income and sales taxes, the property tax is hard for property owners to evade. Moreover, the taxpayer's property provides collateral for his or her tax liability. If property taxes go unpaid, the local government can place a lien on the property in question. The lien prevents the property from being sold or mortgaged until the owner meets his or her tax liability. If collection efforts fail, the local government can ultimately seize and sell the property. The local government retains the taxes owed, as well as penalties, interest, and administrative costs, and remits the remaining amount to the owner. Although local governments typically foreclose on properties only after repeatedly attempting to collect back taxes, the threat of such foreclosure gives property owners a powerful incentive to comply with the law. The difficulty that property owners face in evading the tax clearly helps the government officials that administer it.

The ease of compliance is equally attractive to taxpayers. Most residential property owners face minimal compliance costs. Unlike the much more complicated claims required when taxpayers file federal and state income taxes, taxpayers do not need to fill out any property tax forms. Generally, the government, not the individual, calculates the property tax; the taxpayer's role begins and ends with paying the tax. As a result, individual property owners rarely incur fees for professional tax assistance (i.e., accountants or attorneys) when complying with the property tax. Only the sales tax has similarly light compliance burdens.

As explained in chapter 5, state and local governments provide property-tax exemptions and credits to such groups as poor homeowners, the elderly, disabled residents, and veterans. Such tax benefits, while meant to provide relief, increase compliance costs for individuals and the administrative costs for local governments. But the additional compliance costs have not proved to be particularly onerous to the recipients.

Unlike residential properties, commercial and industrial properties present property tax compliance issues for both government and taxpayers (Strauss 2001). Commercial property is often unique and thus presents administrative problems, particularly with respect to valuation. Local government spends more resources ascertaining commercial property values than determining residential values.

Moreover, commercial property owners generally face significantly higher property tax burdens than do residential property owners. Because of this greater financial stake, businesses have more incentive to question government assessments of their property. Commercial property owners also have the resources to challenge assessments. These greater resources make administering the tax more expensive. The increased administrative and compliance costs of taxing commercial property can drain public resources and distort investment decisions. Cost, compliance, and investment factors have led some scholars to call for legislation that limits the property tax to residential property (see, for example, Break 1980). The taxation of commercial and industrial property, however, is politically attractive because officials and the public tend to view business taxes as "victimless" because they fall on corporations or are exported (Youngman 1999c).

Overall, the local property tax presents few administrative and compliance burdens, particularly with respect to residential property. It is arguably the most efficient tax in terms of administration, with 96 percent of the total tax collected annually, a far higher percentage than for any other type of tax revenue (Shuford and Young 2000). As Fischer (1989, 123) notes,

> A symbiotic relationship between taxation and structure of government exists in the United States. The property tax has evolved into a form well suited to financing of small, overlapping units of government with varying functional responsibilities. Other forms of revenue require greater administrative cooperation or involve varying degrees of control by higher levels of government.

A BENEFITS TAX

The property tax has endured because it is conceptually attractive. Unlike state sales and income taxes, property tax revenue is raised locally to support local public services. Thus, the connection between the source of the revenue (the property) and what is being provided (public services) has stayed strong (Bird 1993; Shuford and Young 2000). That connection arises because the services provided by local governments benefit the owners and renters of the property within the jurisdiction. The property, the taxes, and the services are all linked. That is why, as explained in the preceding chapter, local governments pursue policies that protect and increase the value of property located in their jurisdictions, particularly the value of residential property. The quality of public services is directly related to property values (Fischel 2001b).

But one need not read the extensive academic literature on this subject to understand the connection. A citizen's most valuable asset is usually his or her home. The citizen's wealth increases as the value of the home increases. Quality police and fire protection, paved roads, and schools that score well on standardized tests all contribute to the value of the home. People desire to live in communities that offer quality public services. The resulting demand for such services increases property values in the jurisdiction providing the services.

The beneficiary of the public services is the property owner, and, under the benefit principle of taxation, it is the property owner who should be paying for the services. To the extent the property tax is used to fund local government (i.e., to provide services to those who pay for them), it must be considered a benefit tax (Fischel 2001b). Essentially, the property tax can be viewed as the cost of receiving local government services. The tax cost reflects the value of the services (i.e., benefits) received.

As noted in chapter 3, benefit taxes are the most efficient and effective means of financing local government. Many leading economists have recognized that the property tax is a benefit tax—and thus particularly well suited for financing local government (Bird 1993; Break 1995; Fischel 2001b; Gramlich 1993; Netzer 2001). One of most astute observers of local public finance stated, "Local property taxation, in conjunction with local zoning ordinances, produce what is in effect a system of benefit taxation that promotes efficient local and fiscal decisions on the part of households" (Oates 1999b, 68).

But not everyone agrees that property taxation is a good thing. Some economists contend that the property tax is a tax on capital and that, as such, it can have a progressive or redistributive effect—a belief referred to as the "new view." Some economists argue that property tax burdens result in higher housing prices and are thus regressive (Netzer 1966). Others argue that property taxes are actually progressive taxes on capital (Mieszkowski and Zodrow 1989).[3] According to another line of thinking, property taxes are, in fact, nondistortionary benefit taxes (Fischel 2001b; Hamilton 1975). See Ladd (1998) for a review of the extensive literature in this subject.

The question of the distributional effects of property taxation is more than an academic exercise. If the benefit view is correct, then the anti-property-tax movement may be destructive, because, under this view, the property tax is an integral component of an efficient local public finance sector. On the other hand, if the new view is correct, then the property tax is a tax on capital and not necessarily a good thing. Under the new view, the anti-property-tax movement can be justified on efficiency grounds. But this debate centers on the effects and incidence of the property tax on the national economy. That is, nationally, the property tax may have a progressive effect. But even adherents to the view that property taxes may be progressive recognize that, at the local level, property owners will bear the full burden of tax increases—as one would expect under the benefit view (Zodrow 2001, 144).[4]

In either case, the connection between property taxes and local government services cannot be denied. The American public recognizes this connection and is willing to pay property taxes to support local public services that it desires.

A TAX THAT ALLOWS LOCAL CONTROL

Economist Harold Graves (1948) once noted that the virtue of the property tax is that it is the best available independent source of local revenue and makes it possible for citizens to spend their own money as they collectively see fit. One recent study concluded that local fiscal autonomy is a direct result of reliance on property taxes (Shuford and Young 2000).

The property tax has given local constituencies control over their financial matters (Harris 1974; Knapp 1999). The property tax is the one source of revenue that state and federal governments do not have to legislate, administer, or collect. The property tax has been successful because for the past century it has been used exclusively by local governments.

Arguably, the property tax cannot be efficiently administered by central governments. Attempts to adopt statewide property taxes have been rejected or, when implemented, have caused significant political controversy (Brunori 2001d). The controversy stems from the fact that, although the property tax is tolerated as a local benefit tax, the public largely sees the tax as incapable of redistributing income (Brunori 1999).[5]

Generally speaking, the more levels of government that impose a tax on the same base, the less control each level of government has on that tax. When multiple levels of government tax income, for example, increasing rates becomes politically difficult because the overall income tax burden is already high. When multiple levels of government impose a tax on the same base, altering that base also makes the system more complicated. In the United States, the federal government has traditionally relied on income taxes to fund public services, while the states have traditionally relied on a combination of income and consumption taxes to fund public services. But local governments, except for those in the largest cities, have relied almost exclusively on property taxes.

The property tax has been successful, in part, because neither the federal nor the state governments tax real property. Thus, theoretically, local governments should have greater flexibility with the property tax system than with other major taxes.

A VISIBLE TAX

Another virtue of the property tax is its visibility. Taxpayers know the amount, the frequency, and the purpose of this tax. As noted in chapter 3, visibility ensures accountability (Bird 1993). Unlike sales taxes (which are paid in small increments to vendors) or income taxes (which are generally withheld by employers), property taxes are generally paid in a lump sum to the government. Taxes paid directly to the government are more visible than taxes paid through intermediaries. There is little doubt that the property tax is among the most, and probably the most, visible of taxes encountered by American citizens. Property owners get a bill—at times a large bill—on an annual or biannual basis.[6]

Knowing the exact amount of the tax helps property owners evaluate whether their tax dollars are paying for the services they want and need. This evaluative process is critical for local governments to operate efficiently. As noted in chapter 2, Tiebout assumed that citizens and business leaders would use information about the tax and service levels of competing local governments to decide where to locate their homes and businesses. But more critical to the analysis is that citizens need to have accurate information about the tax costs imposed by their local government. The property tax, which is highly visible, provides that information better than most other revenue sources.

As explained in chapter 5, the high visibility of the property tax also causes much public discontent. Many citizens dislike the tax, especially compared with other levies, because it is a known quantity. Even if unpopular, however, the tax's high visibility allows citizens to evaluate the costs of their government.

Conclusion

The property tax is an important source of revenue because it meets the general requirements of a sound local tax system—it offers an efficient, stable, and fair method of collecting revenue. As Fisher (1996, 210) states, "There are no taxes capable of financing our current system of local governments that can be locally levied and administered, except the property tax."

But the advantages of the tax go beyond the mere ability to raise adequate revenue for local governments. Arguably, the property tax has also helped create the efficiencies inherent in the American federal system of government. Local governments use the property tax to match public services and taxpayers. If, as is widely thought, the efficiencies of localism arise from the fact that local governments are more capable of ascertaining the wishes of their residents, then the property tax only enhances that efficiency.

As one noted scholar has observed, "among many public finance economists it is almost dogma that local government reliance on the local property tax is a good thing" (McGuire 1999, 130). The theoretical virtues of the tax as well as its historical performance support that dogma.

As chapter 5 illustrates, despite the tax's resilience, many problems and obstacles threaten its dominance. Stiff public and political opposition to the property tax persists—even as scholars continue to argue its virtues. As Youngman (1998a, 114) notes, "Economists have long held the property tax in higher regard than does the public at large."

NOTES

1. McGuire (2001) argues that some property tax limitations may be justified because they prevent unchecked growth of tax revenue and government.

2. The administrative problems with the property tax usually relate to valuation issues (Bowman and Mikesell 1978b; Kidd 2002; Lowery 1982; Youngman 1998a). See Walters, Cornia, and Shank (1995) for a discussion of the significant problems regarding property tax administration of public utilities.

3. See also Aaron (1975), who argued that owners of capital bear the burden of property taxes, rendering the tax progressive.

4. In the public arena, political leaders and the media routinely characterize the property tax as regressive, when they actually intend to say unfair or unpopular. As Youngman (2002a) notes, the political perception is not justified on economic grounds.

5. Vermont and New Hampshire, for example, impose statewide real property taxes to fund public school finance. Those policies have sparked intense political controversy (Brunori 2001d).

6. The property tax is generally not considered visible to renters, who bear, usually unknowingly, some of the tax's burdens (Oates 2001a). The tax is also less visible to those who pay their liability through their mortgage payments.

5

The Property Tax under Siege

The property tax has certainly carried the onus of extreme public dislike.
—Alvin Sokolow, 1998

Although the property tax continues to dominate local government finance, its share of total local revenue has steadily declined. Before the Great Depression, the property tax provided two-thirds of all local government revenue (Netzer 1993). Local government reliance on the tax reached its peak in the mid-1970s (Rafool 2002). By 1999, however, the property tax accounted for less than 25 percent of total local government revenue (U.S. Census Bureau 2000). As property tax proceeds have fallen as a percentage of total revenue, the ability of local governments to increase their future reliance on the tax has also declined.

Five broad, interrelated reasons explain the decline in the share of property taxes. First, the tax has long been very unpopular among citizens in general and homeowners in particular. The unpopularity has created significant political opposition to the tax. Second, the property tax system operates in most states under statutory and constitutional limitations regarding rates, assessments, and the amount of revenue that can be raised. These limitations have arisen largely because of the public's unhappiness with the tax. Third, exemptions for charitable organizations and businesses have proliferated. These exemptions have shrunk the property tax base. Fourth, efforts to provide relief to the elderly and to poor homeowners have further limited the tax's revenue-raising potential. Fifth, the increased centralization of the financing of elementary and secondary education has reduced local government's reliance on the property tax. Public education, once almost exclusively paid for by local governments, is increasingly being financed by the states. Centralization has weakened the rationale for taxing property and has further undercut public support for the property tax. Combined, these factors have reduced reliance on the property tax. They also have the potential to further limit the future role of the tax.

Public Unhappiness

It has now become part of public finance lore that the property tax is the "worst tax." It certainly is among the most disliked of taxes. During the latter half the 20th century, the Advisory Commission on Intergovernmental Relations set out to gauge people's views on the federal, state, and local tax systems, including the taxes they most disliked. Each year, respondents named the property tax as either the worst tax or the second-worst tax (after the federal income tax).

Despite the property tax's positive attributes, described in chapter 4, the public has grown to dislike the property tax for several reasons.

Visibility

The tax's high visibility, although a positive attribute by tax theory measures, makes the tax a lightning rod for criticism. The property tax, one of the most visible taxes paid by property owners in the United States, is imposed on a yearly basis, with the property owner receiving a bill from the city or county once or twice a year. The amount due usually exceeds any other single tax payment the property owner must make.[1] This "sticker shock" has contributed to the public's unhappiness with the tax. According to opinion polls, the public consistently lists the two most visible taxes, the property tax and the federal income tax, as their least favorite taxes.

The property tax also spurs dissatisfaction because, unlike the sales tax, the taxpayer does not voluntarily trigger its payment. Rather, ownership of real property results in the tax. Unlike income taxes, the government demands payment even though there may be no additional income from which to pay the tax. In addition, the government bills the property owner directly and requires him or her to pay the tax in a lump sum. In contrast, sales taxes are collected in small amounts from vendors, and income taxes are usually withheld from individuals' paychecks (Youngman 1999b).

As noted in chapter 4, visibility is considered a virtue in a sound tax system. Visibility means that citizens can explicitly ascertain the costs of government. Ironically, while contributing to the public's dislike, high visibility has helped make the local government system efficient. The ability to determine whether the government is providing the desired mix of taxes and services requires that citizens understand their tax burdens. A property tax certainly performs that function. Yet the high visibility has led directly to the unpopularity of the tax, a fact not lost on most public finance experts (Youngman 1999b).

Unfair Administration

The property tax's administration has added to the public's dissatisfaction. In general, property should be assessed on its market value, defined as what a willing buyer would pay a willing seller. More important, all similarly situated property should bear the same relative tax burden. Such horizontal equity is critical to sound tax policy. Imposing different tax burdens on similarly situated taxpayers leads to distrust of the tax system and government (Brunori 2001e).

In reality, however, discrepancies between the assessed and market value of property abound. In fact, many local governments have traditionally failed to meet legal requirements to maintain current market values through timely property reassessments. The result is that property values are often overstated for tax purposes (Strauss 2001). And this treatment has contributed to unhappiness with the property tax.

The problems associated with uneven valuations are heightened because property tax records are public documents and are available for inspection. Thus, property owners can ascertain and compare the assessed value of their neighbor's property. Moreover, the press and researchers continue to investigate the inaccuracy of property tax assessments. Despite great improvements in the accuracy of valuation practices over the past quarter-century, inequities remain, and the system continues to be viewed as unfair by many taxpayers. Moreover, property tax inequities are easier to identify than inequities resulting from the administration of other taxes, making the property tax a ready target for criticism.

Shifting Property Tax Burdens

Property tax burdens have shifted from commercial and industrial real estate to residential real estate. Homeowners are bearing a larger share of the property tax burden than ever before (Green, Chevrin, and Lippard 2002). Several reasons explain this phenomenon. Strauss (2001) attributes the shift to four factors: (1) taxes on many types of business property are difficult to administer; (2) federal tax policy has encouraged investment in equipment rather than in plants; (3) homeownership rates and home values have increased; and (4) economic downturns have kept commercial and industrial property values relatively low.

Another likely factor contributing to the shift is the proliferation of tax incentives meant to foster economic development. These incentives, which usually waive or reduce businesses' property taxes, shift the burden of paying for local government away from business toward homeowners.[2]

The result of this shift in tax burdens has been an increase in the relative amount of property taxes paid by individual property owners, particularly homeowners. The increased tax burdens have not been accompanied by increased or improved public services. The increased tax burdens on homeowners have led to increased public dissatisfaction with the property tax (Strauss 1997).

Consequences of Public Dissatisfaction

The public's dissatisfaction with the property tax has limited the tax's role in the local government finance system. As described in later sections of this chapter, the public's displeasure led directly to the property tax revolts of the 1970s and 1980s. These revolts, in turn, resulted in significant statutory and constitutional limitations on the property tax. Over time, the public's dissatisfaction has also created a strong political bias against the tax.

Many political leaders, seizing on public perceptions, have called for further reductions in the tax and have taken a negative view of the property tax.[3] According to one recent poll, 50 percent of all state legislators think the property tax is unfair (Beamer 2000). A review of news articles published in *State Tax Notes* from January 2002 to July 2002 shows at least 50 instances in which state political leaders have called for additional limitations on, or outright elimination of, the property tax. Such political views facilitate policies designed to limit the property tax.

Tax Limitations

One of the main reasons for the decline in the use of the property tax as a source of local revenue has been the myriad constitutional and statutory limitations placed on the tax, especially during the past quarter-century. The property tax revolts that spanned the late 1970s and the 1980s wreaked havoc on the tax. As of 2002, 44 states had some restrictions on the ability of local governments to impose property taxes. In 33 of those states, the restrictions were substantial. In these states, property tax revenue had shrunk 15 percent or more since the restrictions were implemented. The initiative process, which arose in part out of citizens' unhappiness with the tax, spawned many of the limitations; 58 different ballot initiatives aimed at reducing property taxes were put before voters between 1979 and 1984 (Sexton and Sheffrin 1995).

Property tax limits take several forms. For example, as of 2002, 33 states have imposed property tax rate limitations. These laws prohibit the imposition of rates over a predetermined level. The most notable rate limitation was established in California by Proposition 13 in 1978, which set the maximum property tax rate at 1 percent. Rate limitations hamper local government's ability to use the property tax.

States can also impose property tax revenue limits. As of 2002, 27 states had such limits on the books. These laws prohibit property tax revenue increases from exceeding certain levels. Property tax revenue limitations take two forms. Some states require a reduction in property tax rates if property tax revenues exceed a certain amount. Other states require reductions in property tax assessments when property tax revenues exceed a certain amount. The property tax revenue increase limits vary from 2 percent in Arizona to 15 percent in Delaware.

Property tax revenue limits affect local government fiscal autonomy. The property tax cannot be used to fund increased public service costs, even if those costs rise simply because of inflation. In 15 states, the effect on local government fiscal autonomy is somewhat mitigated by the fact that the limitations can be overridden by a vote of the citizens.

Another six states impose limitations on increases of assessed property values. These limitations prevent the annual property valuation from increasing beyond the established constitutional or statutory limit. For example, in California, property value assessments cannot increase more than 2 percent a year unless the property changes ownership.

Assessment limitations can lead to the continuous undervaluation of property that has not changed ownership. One of the strengths of the property tax is that its revenue increases automatically as property values increase. The costs of public services increase with inflation. The property tax has naturally been capable of raising revenue to meet those rising costs. This attribute of the tax is severely diminished under a system using assessment limitations.[4]

As numerous studies have shown, tax limitations reduce reliance on the property tax nationwide (see, for example, Brown 2000; Cutler, Elmendorf, and Zeckhauser 1999; Dye and McGuire 1997; McCabe and Feiock 2000; Poterba and Rueben 1995; Preston and Ichniowski 1992; Sexton, Sheffrin, and O'Sullivan 1999; Shadbegian 1998, 1999). The amount of property tax revenue forgone as a result of the various limitations falls in the tens of billions of dollars nationwide (O'Sullivan 2000).

It should be noted that in many states, political leaders taking advantage of antitax sentiments have promised to increase state aid to replace lost property tax revenue (Brunori 2001e). Such promises fueled citizen support for the tax limitations, because voters believed service levels would stay the same but that payment would shift from a local to a state responsibility. The increased aid, however, never materialized—at least not to the extent of the lost revenue.

The public's dissatisfaction with the property tax has led to limits being placed on the tax and a continued political bias against strengthening property tax revenues. Although the public's attitude about property taxes may change, the limitations, which are often imposed by constitutional amendment, will be harder to change or eliminate.

A Proliferation of Exemptions

Besides the loss of revenue created by the tax limitation movement, other factors have deterred local governments from relying more heavily on property taxes. Exemptions for charitable organizations and economic development have proliferated over the past half-century. In addition, numerous exemptions exist for farm property and government-owned property. For example, according to Thomas (1991), in many counties,

60 percent of property was tax exempt. These exemptions, which are generally imposed by state governments, cost local governments billions of dollars a year in revenue.[5]

Economic Development Exemptions

The proliferation of tax exemptions in the name of economic development has proved a major challenge to the property tax. State and local governments hoping to attract jobs and business investment grant property tax breaks to companies promising to relocate to or remain in the jurisdiction. Exemptions for property taxes are natural economic development policies (Youngman 1998b). Indeed, property tax exemptions are the most common type of tax incentive offered by local governments.

The amount of money given away every year in the form of property tax incentives is difficult to determine, because most states and local governments do not have tax expenditure reports. According to one recent study, state and local tax incentives totaled $48.8 billion in 1996, with half of that amount attributable to property tax incentives (Thomas 2000). Other, more targeted studies show similar results. In 1996 alone, two Ohio cities combined—Cincinnati and Columbus—offered more than $600 million in property tax abatements to businesses (Thomas 2000).

Notably, when state legislatures adopt property-tax exemptions, state political leaders often promise to reimburse lost revenue to the local government. But rarely do the state governments follow through with enough funds to cover the losses attributable to property tax incentives (Brunori 2001b).

The extensive use of property tax incentives to foster economic development has had a tremendous impact on how much local governments can rely on the tax.

Charitable Exemptions

The value of property held by charities and nonprofit organizations over the past quarter-century has proved another challenge for the property tax. The increased use of charitable exemptions has affected all states and left a whole class of property exempt from taxation—property held by churches, synagogues, schools, charities, universities, and other nonprofits. The total value of charitable property exempt from tax exceeded $990 billion, or about 7 percent of the total real estate values in the

United States in 2000 (Netzer 2002). According to one estimate, the lost property tax revenue owing to charitable exemptions is as high as $13 billion (Cordes, Gantz, and Pollak 2002).[6]

Organizations receiving exemptions use public services that are generally paid for by nonexempt taxpayers. As a result, nonexempt property owners as well as nonproperty owners (through other taxes) face higher tax burdens. This in turn increases the public's unhappiness with the property tax.[7]

To alleviate the impact of lost revenue, most states allow the local governments to accept payments in lieu of taxes (PILOTs) from exempt organizations. PILOTs are voluntary payments made to local governments to defray the costs of public services.[8] But PILOTs are not widely used. In 1998, only 7 of the 51 largest cities in the United States actively solicited PILOTs from exempt nonprofit organizations (Leland 2002). Given their limited use, PILOTs cannot come close to covering the property tax revenue lost through charitable exemptions.[9]

Farm Relief

Another broadly used property-tax exemption applies to farmland. Virtually every state provides property tax relief to farm owners. Initially, the motivation behind such relief was to help preserve the viability of family-owned farms. More recently, many environmentalists have backed farm tax relief to slow urban and suburban sprawl.

In 44 states, farm tax relief primarily takes the form of preferential assessments. In other words, farmland is valued at its current use, rather than at market value. In many instances, the market value of a swath of farmland, particularly in areas near metropolitan areas, far surpasses the current-use value. Except in two of the states offering preferential assessments (Michigan and Wisconsin), these programs are not tied to income, and they benefit all owners of farmland. Studies show that tax relief programs have had little impact on the goal of preserving family farms or preventing urban sprawl (see, for example, Vitaliano 1999).

Government Property

A significant amount of property is exempt from local tax because either the federal or a state government owns it. Although the exact amount of such property is difficult to ascertain, it is likely in the hundreds of billions of dollars nationwide.[10] Virtually all government-owned property is exempt from tax under the Supremacy Clause of the U.S. Constitution. The policy rationale for exempting government property is that such exemptions reduce the costs of government (Swain 2000). Federal and state governments often make PILOTs to compensate for lost revenue. But these payments generally do not cover the revenue lost from the exempt property.

Tax Relief Measures

A recent New Jersey study found that the poorest 20 percent of homeowners bore a relative property tax burden four times as great as the wealthiest 1 percent of homeowners (Coleman, Hughes, and Kehler 2001). An earlier single-year study found that the property tax was regressive for younger households and even more so for elderly households (Reschovsky 1994). Reschovsky, however, also found that, when studied over a 12-year period, the property tax for younger households was proportional. These studies can be added to the ongoing debate, discussed in chapter 4, as to which groups ultimately bear the burden of the property tax.

Despite this debate, there is a perception that the property tax unfairly burdens low- and moderate-income homeowners, particularly elderly homeowners (Youngman 1999c). For that reason, state governments have instituted various programs to relieve homeowners' property tax burdens through homestead exemptions, homestead credits and circuit breakers, and property tax deferrals.

Homestead Exemptions

Twenty-eight states and the District of Columbia grant homestead reductions, that is, reductions in the amount of assessed value subject to taxation for owner-occupied housing. In effect, all homeowners in these states benefit from homestead exemptions. In four states (Nebraska, North Dakota, Ohio, and Washington), however, the exemption phases out as income increases. Homestead exemptions are based on the political belief that homeownership benefits the community and society (Youngman 1996).

Homestead exemptions are generally mandated by state law, with most states requiring local governments to absorb the costs of the exemption. Indeed, only 12 states reimburse local governments for some or all of the costs of the exemption.[11]

Homestead Credits and Circuit Breakers

In addition to homestead exemptions, many states provide credits directly to homeowners, and in many cases renters, to alleviate the burdens of property tax liability. The credits are generally the same for all eligible households in a particular jurisdiction, and they typically take the form of circuit breakers. Thirty states and the District of Columbia use circuit breakers. States offer tax credits to low- and moderate-income homeowners; 26 states offer such relief to renters. Four states provide circuit-breaker relief only to homeowners.

Circuit breakers generally involve setting an income threshold that property tax liability cannot exceed. Homeowners and renters with property tax burdens exceeding the threshold receive the tax credits directly from the state. One-third of the states provide the relief in the form of income tax credits.

The advantage of using circuit breakers, as opposed to homestead exemptions, is that the state, rather than the local government, incurs the cost of the credits. Circuit breakers enable the state to target relief to those who need it most. A fully refundable credit makes the state income tax more progressive even in states with flat income tax rates.

Property Tax Deferrals

One of the most effective, and underused, methods of providing property tax relief is through deferrals. Twenty-two states and the District of Columbia allow the elderly and disabled to defer property tax payments until the homes are sold or the taxpayer dies. The deferred property taxes become liens against the value of the property. Local governments generally charge interest on the amount of tax liability deferred. When the property is sold or the homeowner dies, the local government collects the unpaid property tax and any interest accrued.

Property tax deferrals are less expensive than homestead exemptions or circuit breakers. But as Youngman (2002b) notes, deferrals are underused. In 2001, only 10 senior citizens in Boston took advantage of such deferrals. And nationwide, only 1 out of 72 eligible households requested deferrals.

Although the elderly generally do not like tax liens on their property, this group often has liens placed on their homes through second mortgages, home equity loans, and reverse mortgages. Thus, educating elderly homeowners about the benefits of tax deferral may lead to increased usage.

The Case of School Finance

The ongoing school finance crisis has further limited government reliance on property taxes. Traditionally, paying for elementary and secondary school education was primarily the responsibility of local governments. In meeting this obligation, local governments relied almost exclusively on the property tax. Of course, some wealthier jurisdictions had a much larger property tax base, allowing them to pay more for teachers, buildings, computers, and other resources than poorer communities.[12] Consequently, wealthier communities could spend more money per capita on their children's education than could poorer cities and counties. That greater spending often translated into better schools.[13]

In the past quarter-century, advocates for poor school districts have increasingly challenged the inequality of public education finance. In a 1971 landmark ruling, *Serrano v. Priest*, the California Supreme Court declared the state's public school finance system illegal under the state constitution. By 2001, citizens had challenged the constitutionality of using property taxes to finance education in 43 states. As of 2002, courts in 19 states have declared it illegal to use the local property tax as the primary means of paying for schools.

Courts have ordered states to "equalize" funding of schools between rich and poor communities. The states have usually reacted by earmarking certain statewide taxes to pay for public schools. For example, Michigan imposed an additional 1 percent statewide sales tax to pay for virtually all public school expenses (and tied that tax increase to a dramatic cut in the property tax). In 1999, New Hampshire adopted a statewide property tax. The tax was collected locally, remitted to the state, and then redistributed to poorer communities. In 1997, Vermont, through Act 60, imposed a similar statewide property tax, which required localities to remit a portion of property tax revenue to the state for redistribution. In 1993, Texas enacted the so-called Robin Hood law, which required wealthier school districts to remit a portion of their revenue to the state for redistribution to the poor.

The shift to statewide property taxes has proved politically divisive (Brunori 2001b). The political controversies stem from the fact that the property tax can fund local governments, but it generally fails as a means of redistributing wealth.

As a result of the increased centralization of school finance, the use of property taxes in general has decreased. As Fischel (1989) notes, the property tax was acceptable as a vehicle for funding local education. Once the property tax was no longer the primary means of financing education, public support for the tax, meager to begin with, evaporated. Fischel asserts that the school finance litigation helped cause the property tax revolts, particularly in the case of California's Proposition 13. The *Serrano* court ordered sweeping reforms for the California education finance system, which resulted in redistributing wealth from high-spending school districts to lower-spending jurisdictions. According to Fischel, the *Serrano* case changed the property tax from a benefits tax to a vehicle for the statewide redistribution of wealth.

Under Fischel's hypothesis, voters in wealthier school districts voiced their displeasure with the redistributive effects of *Serrano* by supporting Proposition 13. This theory has been widely accepted by scholars, and its contribution to the understanding of Proposition 13 cannot be denied. Fischel's theory is consistent with the notion that education finance reform efforts draw much support from antitax activists who see the movement to centralize education finance as a means of lowering overall tax burdens (see, generally, Youngman 1997b).

State centralization of school finance has reduced reliance on the property tax. State funding of schools has also made it more difficult for local governments to raise taxes in general, and property taxes in particular (Bowman, MacManus, and Mikesell 1992). Research by Bahl, Sjoquist, and Williams (1990) shows that school finance litigation has led directly to decreased reliance on the property tax. Less reliance on the tax means policymakers have less rationale for supporting the property tax (see Break 1995, 2000; Sexton and Sheffrin 1995; Sokolow 1998).

School financing reform has profoundly affected the property tax. As Sheffrin (1999) notes,

> School finance litigation is the single most important factor affecting property tax today. It ultimately undercuts the rationale for the property tax as a truly local tax. In my view, homeowners were willing to pay higher property taxes if they were convinced that this would lead to quality schools. The school finance litigation movement essentially breaks this tie.

Conclusion

The property tax has faced many challenges and problems in recent decades. Intense public dissatisfaction with the tax has translated, not surprisingly, into widespread political opposition. The tax limitation movement has curtailed the use of the tax by local governments. Economic development and charitable exemptions have shrunk the tax base. And efforts to equalize school finance have diminished public and political support for the tax.

The extensive political and legal limitations on the property tax are not likely to be rescinded in the near future. Accordingly, it will be difficult for local governments to rely more heavily on the property tax. The next three chapters look at the other taxes that local governments could potentially tap to finance public services.

NOTES

1. For property owners who pay the tax as part of their mortgage, the property tax is less visible. The amount provided to the mortgage holder is higher because of the tax liability, but the amount dedicated to taxes is not readily apparent. This is one reason why the elderly, who are less likely to have mortgaged property, are more opposed to property taxes.

2. The shift to a service economy, which has placed increasing emphasis on intangible property as opposed to traditional plant and heavy equipment, may also have contributed to the shifting burden (Strauss 1997). See chapter 9 for a discussion of the effects of the changing economy on the property tax.

3. For example, political leaders in Arkansas have pushed to abolish the property tax and replace it with a statewide sales tax. This movement continued despite studies showing that such reforms would have a detrimental effect on government services and the state's economy (Veasey and Hy 2000).

4. In addition, eight states impose general expenditure limits and two states impose general revenue limits on local governments. These limitations are not specifically tied to property taxes, but they still limit local fiscal autonomy.

5. California is a good example. One study found that 68 different classes of property, ranging from parking facilities at places of worship to property owned by volunteer fire departments, are exempt from the property tax in California (Micheli 2001).

6. Because the study mentioned excluded property owned by religious organizations (which own an estimated one-half of the total exempt property in the United States), the total loss of property tax revenue is probably considerably greater (Cordes et al. 2002).

7. The Urban Institute and the Lincoln Institute of Land Policy held a major national conference to address the problem of charitable exemptions. The conference culminated in a widely regarded book on the subject (Brody 2002).

8. While payments in lieu of taxes are voluntary, they are often made as a result of threats by local governments. Some governments will threaten to withhold building permits or to formally challenge an organization's exempt status (Steinberg and Bilodeau 1999).

9. Another problem with exemptions for charitable organizations is that they complicate the local tax system. Determining which organizations are entitled to exemptions is a difficult task under many states' tax laws (Brunori 2001c; Youngman 2000). For example, in 2002 the Texas legislature expanded the breadth of charitable exemption to property owned by organizations "primarily" engaged in charitable work. The earlier law provided exemptions only to property owned by organizations engaged "exclusively" in charitable work. This broadening of the scope of eligibility created much uncertainty among local governments and charitable organizations. It also opened up the possibility that many more organizations would apply for exemptions. The potential loss of property tax revenue troubled local governments (Croteau 2002).

10. In Virginia alone, federal- and state-owned property was valued at $44.3 billion (Report of the Commission on Virginia's State and Local Tax Structure for the 21st Century 2000).

11. The states that reimburse local governments for the costs of homestead exemptions are California, Indiana, Iowa, Louisiana, Maine, Massachusetts, New Jersey, North Carolina, North Dakota, Oklahoma, South Carolina, and Wyoming.

12. Many leading U.S. economists have researched the issue of fiscal inequities (see Anderson 1994).

13. The problem of fiscal disparities is not an indictment of the property tax, but rather an indictment of local taxing authority. Indeed, such noted economists as Therese J. McGuire of the University of Illinois have indicated that local-option sales and income taxes result in similar, or at times greater, disparities between rich and poor jurisdictions (McGuire 2001).

6

Local-Option Sales and Excise Taxes

In regard to the use of the general sales tax in an urban area, I would be hard pressed to find a reason why this should be done.

—Robert Wassmer, 1998

The increasing costs of local government services and the continuing efforts to limit property taxes have forced local governments to rely more heavily on alternative revenue sources. Two types of consumption taxes imposed by local governments, local-option sales taxes and excise taxes, generate billions of dollars in revenue. This chapter describes each tax and its policy implications.

Local-Option Sales Taxes

After the property tax, local-option sales taxes are the most important source of tax revenue for local governments. These taxes are widely used; 33 of the 45 states imposing a sales tax allow their local governments to impose similar taxes. Even Alaska, which levies no statewide sales tax, allows its local governments to collect local-option sales taxes. Of the 33 states that allow local-option sales taxes, 23 allow both cities and counties to impose the tax. Ten states are evenly split between allowing only cities or only counties to tax sales. Nine other states allow transit authorities or school districts to impose local-option sales taxes.

In 2002, 7,411 local governments, or about 8 percent of all local governments in the United States, imposed local-option sales taxes. The tax is imposed in 4,696 municipalities, 1,602 counties, and 1,113 special districts.[1]

Over the past several decades, local-option sales taxes have grown as a percentage of local tax revenue. In 1977, local governments raised about $5.4 billion, or 7 percent of their total tax revenue, from local-option sales taxes. In 1999, local governments raised about $36 billion from local-option sales taxes, which accounted for about 11 percent of total local government tax revenue (U.S. Census Bureau 2000).

The increased importance of local-option sales taxes is a direct result of the limitations placed on property taxes. A review of census data shows that the amount of revenue raised from local-option sales taxes in the years following Proposition 13 steadily increased. But local-option sales tax revenue has not changed significantly as a percentage of total revenue. In 1997, the tax accounted for about 3 percent of total local revenue, a percentage that has not changed significantly in 40 years. Local-option sales tax growth can be seen, in part, as an attempt to shore up local budgets constrained by the property tax limitations.[2] But local governments have relied more heavily on intergovernmental aid and user fees than on local-option sales taxes in their efforts to replace lost property tax revenue.

Policy Reasons for Imposing Local-Option Sales Taxes

PROMOTING LOCAL AUTONOMY

The local-option sales tax is a direct source of revenue that helps local governments maintain some autonomy over their fiscal affairs. Local control over the tax, however, is limited. In most states, local governments have the authority, within legislatively determined limits, to establish the rates for their local-option sales taxes, but they generally do not have the authority to alter the tax base (i.e., the goods and services subject to the tax). But even in the states that allow local government control over rates, the autonomy is limited. In most states allowing local-option sales taxes, local governments do not have authority to alter the sales tax base. This limitation prohibits local governments from raising additional revenue by subjecting more goods and services to tax when they are unable to increase rates.

In California and Virginia, local governments have no control over the rate or base of the local-option sales tax. In both states, the rate and base are established by the legislature and cannot be modified by the local governments. In Virginia, for example, the state mandates a 1 percent sales tax for the benefit of its local governments. The state collects the tax as part of the statewide sales tax and returns a portion of the revenue to the localities in which the sales were made. In such situations, the local sales tax operates essentially as an intergovernmental transfer of revenue.

Even in states in which local governments have limited control over the rates and base, the tax serves as a continuous source of revenue that can be spent, within broad limits, by the local governments. This source of revenue provides a measure of autonomy, because the local sales tax revenue is not dependent on yearly appropriations by the state legislature.

ADMINISTRATIVE EFFICIENCY

Local-option sales taxes present only modest administrative and compliance costs for government and taxpayers. In almost all cases, the tax is imposed as part of the state sales tax. In most states, the local-option sales tax is added to the state sales tax, and the vendor collects both taxes at the time of purchase. The vendor then remits the total amount of the tax to the state. Finally, the state returns the local portion of the tax receipts to the localities. Local governments have few administrative responsibilities and incur almost no costs as a result of the local-option sales tax. The states are responsible for virtually all aspects of administering the tax, including auditing and enforcing collection.

Residents incur no direct compliance costs from the tax. The consumer's only responsibility is to pay the tax at the time of purchase. The vendor is responsible for recording the tax information and filing the appropriate forms with the Internal Revenue Service. For vendors, the overlap in how they collect and report both the local and state sales taxes offsets this compliance burden. In every state except Alaska, vendors collecting local sales taxes collect state sales taxes at the same time. Moreover, the tax bases for both state and local sales taxes are usually identical. Thus, the marginal costs of compliance are generally considered minimal. The administration and enforcement of the local-option sales tax does have some problems. For example, tax complexity arises when vendors make sales to customers purchasing goods from a different local jurisdiction in the same state. Sales to other jurisdictions may be subject to tax in the jurisdiction of the customer, or depending on the state, the jurisdiction of the vendor (see McLure 2001).

In addition, in several states, local government sales tax bases do not fully conform with the state tax base. For example, Colorado, Georgia, and North Carolina allow local governments to tax certain products that are exempt from state taxes. In these states, retailers must determine which goods and services are subject to local taxation as well as which goods are subject to state taxation. This step adds to the complexity and costs of compliance. Local sales tax systems that do not conform to the state's system also make it more difficult for consumers to ascertain what is and is not subject to the tax.

Moreover, the existence of multiple local-option tax rates in the states complicates compliance, particularly with respect to remote vendors. Only one state authorizing local-option sales taxes requires a uniform rate, and 12 states impose 10 or more different rates (Cornia et al. 2000).[3]

Louisiana and Alabama allow local governments to administer their taxes separately from the state sales tax system. Retailers in those states are subject to additional filing requirements, as well as to the possibility of being audited by multiple levels of government. In these states, compliance and administrative costs are much higher than in states that use a single system to administer the two taxes (National Conference of State Legislatures [NCSL] 1997a).

DIVERSIFICATION OF THE TAX BASE

In addition to raising revenue, local-option sales taxes help diversify the tax base. As many public finance experts have long recognized, a diverse tax base enhances the stability and reliability of the revenue system (NCSL 1992). Diverse systems of revenue allow governments to cope with changing economic conditions. Income taxes, for example, produce more revenue than other taxes during economic expansion but not during recessions. Sales taxes, by contrast, tend to be relatively consistent during economic swings. Moreover, local-option sales taxes allow governments to ease reliance on other taxes, particularly the property tax. Such taxes also allow governments to rely less on intergovernmental aid, a revenue source outside their control (see chapter 8).

PUBLIC ACCEPTANCE

Another advantage of the local-option sales tax is that the public widely accepts the tax. The property tax may be considered the "worst" tax, but the sales tax is considered among the "best" taxes. In opinion polls on attitudes toward taxation, the public consistently identifies the state sales tax as the least objectionable U.S. tax (see, for example, Kincaid and Cole 2001). This favorable rating would likely extend to the local-option sales tax, a levy similar in concept and in administration to the state sales tax.

Since being implemented during the Great Depression, the sales tax has become a routine part of consumers' lives. Only five states do not tax sales; together, these states make up a mere 3 percent of the U.S. population. Thus, most Americans pay sales tax on retail purchases of (mostly nonessential) tangible goods. The widespread acceptance of the sales tax makes the tax stable and predictable, two features tax experts often say are necessary for a sound tax system.

The public also accepts the tax because it is consistent with notions of a free market. Citizens feel in control of their tax burden since they choose whether to purchase goods and services subject to the tax (Brunori 2001e).

The public's acceptance of the sales tax has led to a political bias in favor of the tax, at least at the state level. For example, states experiencing budget problems have routinely raised sales tax rates or expanded the sales tax base in lieu of increasing income or business tax burdens. In times of surplus, however, states have not given consumers a sales tax break. Rather, during periods of economic boom, states have reduced personal income tax burdens more than any other type of tax, including the sales tax (Brunori 2001e). This bias causes state political leaders to allow local governments to use sales taxes more than any other type of own-source revenue.

Problems with Local-Option Sales Taxes

The use of the local-option sales taxes has many political and administrative advantages. But many problems also plague the tax, leading one noted economist to declare that the local-option sales tax is in danger of becoming "irrelevant" (Break 2000, 768).

SHRINKING TAX BASE
Most significantly, like the state sales tax, local-option sales taxes suffer from a shrinking tax base. The sales tax base has been steadily decreasing relative to the overall economy (Boyd 2000). The decrease primarily reflects the continued shift from a manufacturing- to a service-based economy (Knapp 1999). Services and intangible property generally are not subject to sales tax.

The debacle over electronic commerce has also lessened the effectiveness of, and consequently the interest in, local-option sales taxes. State and local governments stand to lose billions of dollars in sales tax revenue as consumers increase their Internet and mail-order purchases (see, for example, Bruce and Fox 2001b). According to a widely cited study, the effects of electronic commerce could cost state and local governments an estimated $54.8 billion by 2011 (Bruce and Fox 2001b).

Even when local governments manage to collect the tax from multistate transactions, compliance can be particularly burdensome for the remote sellers. The vendors must identify the local jurisdiction, determine whether the transaction is subject to tax, calculate the tax, and collect and remit the tax to the jurisdiction in question. Because of these compliance difficulties, electronic commerce poses a significant threat to local-option sales taxes (Bonnet 1998).

Unlike when the tax was first implemented in the 1930s, most of what Americans consume now is not subject to sales tax. Most observers believe that the problems posed by a shrinking tax base will continue (Fox 1998; Mikesell 1998).

INTERJURISDICTION COMPETITION

Local-option sales taxes are widely considered inefficient methods of collecting tax in a competitive inter-local government system. Because local-option sales taxes increase the costs of consumption, citizens have an incentive to shop in cities and towns that offer lower overall tax burdens. Thus, jurisdictions that impose local-option sales taxes could eventually see their residents shopping in towns and cities with no or relatively low sales taxes (see, for example, Wassmer 1998). This possibility keeps local governments from imposing sales tax burdens that are out of line with those of neighboring jurisdictions. In addition, businesses lobby to keep local-option sales taxes as low as possible. And businesses in no- or low-tax jurisdictions use the tax advantages to attract customers.

Another problem with local-option sales taxes is that, once in place, they often spur competition for retail development (Lewis 2001). When states restrict local governments' ability to use property tax revenue, local governments often turn to the local sales tax. This reliance leads many communities to encourage the building of retail shopping space to enhance their revenues. As a result, many communities see a large growth in the number of shopping malls and large retail stores. Ironically, local governments often compete to attract retail development by offering property tax incentives. Such incentives further weaken the property tax base, which in turn forces local governments to seek alternative sources of revenue, such as the local-option sales tax.

Once retailers have located within a jurisdiction, they become the most ardent opponents of local-option sales taxes. Such taxes add to the over-all cost of purchasing products or services they sell. There is a perception among retailers that local-option sales taxes will make retailers less competitive compared with businesses in areas with no or fairly low taxes.

REGRESSIVITY

Local-option sales taxes, like their state counterparts,[4] are regressive—that is, poorer residents pay a larger percentage of their income in local-option sales taxes than wealthier residents. This imbalance is especially evident in localities that continue to tax such necessities as food, medicine, and utilities. Governments should minimize the use of regressive taxes (see citations in Brunori 2001e). Together, state and local sales taxes increase the overall regressivity of the revenue system. One North Carolina study, for example, found that increased local-option income taxes burdened the least affluent 20 percent of citizens six times more than the most affluent 1 percent (Gardner 1999).

Attempts to alleviate regressivity have actually weakened the sales tax as a source of revenue for both state and local governments (Brunori 2001e). State political leaders, recognizing the inherent regressivity of the tax, have exempted most goods and services deemed necessities, such as food for home consumption, prescription medicine, utilities, and, in some states, clothing. Such state exemptions, which generally apply in localities, relieve the burden on the poor but shrink the potential tax base.

REDUCED STATE FLEXIBILITY/HIGHER FEDERAL TAXES

Another problem with the local-option sales tax is that it reduces state governments' flexibility in using the state sales tax. The problems posed by multiple levels of government taxing the same base make it less likely that political leaders will support additional local sales taxing authority. According to many economists and public finance experts, the efficiency and effectiveness of a tax decline when multiple levels of government tax the same base. Sobel (1997), for example, finds that when two levels of government tax the same base, the combined tax rate tends to be inefficiently large. Neither government has an incentive to take the other's tax system into account.

Local-option sales taxes also restrict states' ability to provide tax relief, particularly to low-income taxpayers. Local governments that become heavily dependent on local-option sales taxes oppose efforts to shrink the state sales tax base by exempting necessities. For example, both North Carolina and Virginia ended their sales tax on groceries, but because of financial pressures on the local governments, they did not remove groceries from the local-option sales tax base.

Heavy reliance on local-option sales taxes can also affect federal tax liabilities. Sales taxes, unlike property and income taxes, are not deductible from federal taxable income. Thus, greater reliance on sales taxes, when coupled with lesser reliance on property and income taxes, increases federal tax liability for citizens who itemize their taxes.

FISCAL DISPARITIES

A growing concern with local-option sales taxes is that they create or exacerbate fiscal disparities between wealthy and poorer jurisdictions (McGuire 2001). Bowman and Mikesell (1978), for example, found that tax base disparities under the sales taxes (as well as under the income tax) are larger than under property taxes. Local governments with high concentrations of retail stores, usually located in metropolitan areas, benefit the most from local-option sales taxes. Rural communities, with less commercial and retail activity, benefit the least, because residents tend to shop and pay the local-option sales tax in urban areas. Some evidence suggests that urban areas, particularly large cities, will fight to retain local-option sales taxing authority because of the substantial revenue such authority raises, with much of the revenue coming from nonresidents (Brunori 2001a).

Outlook for Local-Option Sales Taxes

State lawmakers have increasingly opposed new or enhanced local-option sales taxes throughout the United States. In 2001, for example, legislatures in Virginia, North Carolina, Montana, Maine, and New Hampshire rejected efforts to allow or expand local-option sales tax authority, primarily because the business community joined with rural jurisdictions to oppose the measures (Brunori 2001d).

Some states have also tried to repeal local-option sales taxes. For example, in Iowa, rural communities sought to repeal the local-option sales tax authority and replace it with a 1-percentage-point addition to the statewide sales tax; the revenue from the added tax would be distributed across the state. Rural communities vigorously supported the statewide levy. Urban areas, however, successfully lobbied to defeat the measure (Brunori 2001a).

In addition, the ongoing debate over electronic commerce and remote sales has diminished interest in local-option sales taxes. The inability of local governments to collect sales and use tax from out-of-state vendors has led local government officials to request sales tax authority less frequently. At the same time, the business community vigorously opposes expanding local-option taxing authority.

Local-option sales taxes are not likely to become a more significant source of local government revenue. More likely, after adjusting for population growth and inflation, long-term local-option sales tax growth will be negative (Hawkins 2002). Local-option sales taxes are not an effective substitute for property taxes (see, for example, Jung 2001). Although sales taxes will remain a part of the local government finance system, many local governments have fully exploited this revenue source, and the tax is unlikely to increase in importance relative to other taxes or to nontax revenue (Knapp 1999; Wassmer 1998).

Local-Option Excise Taxes

Local-option excise taxes are another source of revenue for local governments. Taxes on hotel lodging and meals are the two main excises imposed by local governments. But some local governments also tax tobacco products and fuel. Sales taxes and excise taxes differ in two important ways. First, sales taxes have general applicability; they are imposed on all goods and services except those specifically exempted from the tax. Excise taxes are imposed only on designated items.

Second, sales taxes are ad valorem taxes. In other words, they derive from the value of the product sold. Excise taxes are often imposed on a per unit basis (e.g., by pack of cigarettes or gallon of gasoline). Sales taxes, which increase with inflation, are likely to grow much faster than excise taxes. During times of economic growth, sales tax revenue increases without raising rates. Excise tax revenue, however, can increase only through increased consumption of the underlying good or through rate increases.

In 1997, local governments raised $13 billion, or 1 percent of their total revenue (tax and nontax revenue combined), from various local-option excise taxes. Excise taxes accounted for about 3 percent of local government tax revenue (U.S. Census Bureau 1998).

Lodging Taxes

Forty-three states allow all or some local jurisdictions to tax short-term overnight accommodations.[5] Even in Alaska, Montana, and Oregon—states without general sales taxes—local jurisdictions have the authority to tax overnight lodging. Thirty-one states allow both county and municipal governments to impose the tax. And seven states allow special districts to tax lodging (NCSL 1997a). Lodging taxes are considered excise taxes because they are imposed on a specific service. These taxes, however, are levied as a percentage of the cost of the accommodations rather than on a per unit basis.

The popularity of lodging taxes can be attributed to a number of factors. Most important, because most hotel and motel patrons reside outside the jurisdictions, lodging taxes allow local jurisdictions to export tax burdens to nonresidents. As noted in chapter 3, although exporting tax burdens conflicts with sound tax policy principles, political leaders widely favor policies that benefit constituents without increasing their tax burdens.

Lodging taxes do present some problems, however. Because they are imposed in addition to state and local sales taxes, the combined tax rates are often very high. Nationally, the combined state and local rate averages 10 percent. But in Washington, Ohio, and California, the overnight lodging tax rates are 14 percent (NCSL 1997a). The lodging tax makes consuming hotel and motel services more expensive. At some point, travelers faced with above-average excises will look for lodging in other localities. Thus, local governments are constrained in their ability to increase lodging taxes.

Lodging taxes can also add to fiscal disparities. Local governments in large cities and vacation areas have the most to gain from lodging taxes. Other local governments see much lower revenue yields from lodging taxes. This difference adds to existing fiscal disparities between urban and rural areas.

Lodging taxes tend to grow more rapidly than most other local excise taxes, in part because the tax is imposed on the value of the accommodations, not on a per room basis. Thus, as inflation pushes up the cost of lodging, tax revenue naturally grows without requiring rate hikes. However, lodging tax revenues are also more susceptible than other excise revenues to economic downturns. When the economy slows, both business and vacation travel falls. This reduction, in turn, shrinks lodging tax revenue.

Meals Taxes

Twenty-seven states allow local jurisdictions to impose a tax on the value of prepared food and beverages.[6] Like lodging taxes, meals taxes are considered excise taxes, because they are imposed on a specific product and service. Meals taxes are also imposed on the value of the meals purchased. Allowable rates vary widely, from a low of 0.5 percent in Los Angeles to a high of 9 percent in many New Jersey jurisdictions. In many states, the local meals tax is levied in addition to state sales taxes.

Meals taxes were once touted by progressives as a luxury tax, because mostly wealthy people ate at restaurants. But today more lower- and middle-income taxpayers eat out on a regular basis than ever before, making the meals tax less progressive.

Like the lodging tax, the meals tax is politically attractive because it allows local governments to export some of the tax burden to nonresidents. In most areas, because residents tend to dine out locally, the meals tax falls more heavily on residents than the lodging tax does. Still, some of the tax, especially in metropolitan and vacation areas, gets exported.

Like the lodgings tax, the meals tax is imposed on top of state and local-option sales taxes. The combined tax rates increase the cost of dining out and limit how much local governments can tax meals. At a certain rate level, citizens will decide to eat at home or go to another, lower-tax location.

Fuel Excise Taxes

Fourteen states allow local governments to impose excise taxes on the purchase of gasoline and diesel fuel. In 1997, local governments raised $880 million, or less than 1 percent of their total tax revenue, from taxing fuel. Nine states allow all local jurisdictions to tax gasoline, while the remaining five limit the tax to specified localities.

Taxing fuel raises a number of policy issues. First, gasoline and diesel fuel taxes exacerbate fiscal disparities among local governments. Localities along major highway systems are likely to raise substantially more revenue from fuel excise taxes than localities farther away from such systems. Moreover, the localities along major highway systems can more easily export the fuel tax burdens to travelers who live outside the jurisdiction.

It is not clear whether local-option fuel taxes spur inefficient tax competition among localities. Most observers do not believe that such taxes seriously affect competition because state limitations on local-option fuel taxes keep rates so low.

While the average rates may be low, local-option fuel taxes do add to the cost of fuel. This reduces state flexibility with respect to fuel taxes. Local-option fuel taxes add to the regressivity of state fuel excise taxes. One problem with fuel excise taxes is they are not likely to keep pace with inflation, because they are imposed on a per unit basis (i.e., by the gallon). To increase local-option fuel tax revenues, either more fuel must be sold or fuel tax rates must increase. Neither option is likely in the foreseeable future.

Local-Option Real Estate Transfer Taxes

Eleven states and the District of Columbia allow local governments to impose real estate transfer taxes.[7] Such taxes take the form of excises imposed at the time real estate is transferred or recorded for sale and are generally based on the sales price of the real estate.

Local-option real estate transfer taxes do not raise significant amounts of revenue for local governments. However, they are among the most politically controversial types of levies available to local governments. In particular, the real estate industry strongly opposes such taxes, because it believes the tax deters real estate sales. For this reason, realtor associations lobby strenuously against the tax. In addition, because the tax raises relatively little revenue but stirs much opposition, it is unlikely to play a significant role in the future of local government finance.

Local-Option Tobacco Taxes

Ten states authorize local governments to impose excise taxes on cigarettes. (One state, New York, only gives New York City authority to tax cigarettes.) However, in two of these 10 states—Arkansas and Idaho—no local governments impose the tax. In 1997, local governments together raised $180 million in cigarette excise taxes, a tiny fraction of total tax revenue (U.S. Census Bureau 1998).

The most obvious policy issue presented by local-option cigarette taxes is the effect on competition among governments. Retailers and convenience stores in jurisdictions with local-option cigarette taxes are particularly concerned given the recent increases in cigarette prices (largely because states have imposed significantly higher excise taxes). The problem for localities imposing these taxes is consumers can purchase cigarettes in nearby, lower-tax jurisdictions. This is especially true in metropolitan areas, since citizens may not need to travel far to find lower-taxed cigarettes.[8]

Cigarette tax revenue is not likely to grow as a source of revenue for local governments. Because cigarette taxes, like gasoline taxes, are imposed on a per unit (i.e., per pack) basis, cigarette tax revenue does not grow with inflation. Thus, the only way local-option cigarette tax revenue can keep pace with inflation is if rates are raised or more cigarettes are purchased in the jurisdiction. But the dangers of cigarette consumption continue to shrink sales in the United States. Increased rates will only provide an incentive to purchase cigarettes outside the taxing jurisdiction.

Conclusion

Sales and excise taxes, despite being reliable sources of local revenue, are not adequate alternatives to the property tax (see Sheffrin 1998). These taxes are beset by their own structural and political problems that, in some cases, could threaten their existence in the modern economy.

Except in the largest cities and vacation areas, local governments will likely rely less on general sales taxes in the future. The sales tax faces several problems, including a shrinking base, collection issues for remote sales, and growing concerns over fiscal disparities. Thus, the local-option sales tax is unlikely to play a meaningful future role in financing local government.

Local governments will also rely less on excise taxes. Lodging and meals taxes will remain a constant, if small, part of the local government finance system, especially in areas where the burden of paying the taxes can be exported to nonresidents.

NOTES

1. The number of local governments imposing local-option sales taxes was obtained from a variety of sources, including state department of revenue web sites, the Federation of Tax Administrators, and *State Tax Notes* magazine. The numbers vary over time as local governments elect to use or discontinue the tax.

2. Following the property tax revolts, the number of states with local-option sales taxes increased significantly. In 1970, 23 states authorized local-option sales taxes. By 2002, 33 states allowed local governments some authority to tax sales.

3. Solving the problem of multiple rates is a difficult task (Cornia et al. 2000). In many jurisdictions, local-option sales tax revenue is earmarked for particular programs or debt service that significantly increases the costs of simplification. The loss of financial authority will also lead to local government opposition to such reforms.

4. For a discussion of state sales tax issues, including regressivity, see Brunori (2001e).

5. The use of lodging taxes actually occurs nationwide. The seven states that do not allow local-option lodging taxes impose the same tax at the state level.

6. In addition to meals taxes, seven states allow local governments to impose taxes on alcoholic beverages. But total revenue from alcohol taxes ($330 million in 1997) was less than one-third of 1 percent of total local revenue.

7. The states that allow local-option real estate transfer taxes are California, Delaware, Florida, Illinois, Maryland, Nevada, New York, Pennsylvania, Ohio, South Carolina, and Virginia.

8. Another policy concern heard mostly on the state side is that cigarette taxes are regressive. Poorer smokers pay a larger portion of their income in cigarette taxes than wealthier smokers.

7

Income and Business Taxes

Local income taxes will be limited by household mobility. If a city imposes an income tax when neighboring communities do not, it can anticipate an outflow of residents.
—Steven Sheffrin, 1998

In addition to the consumption taxes described in chapter 6, many local governments impose levies on personal income and wages. Local governments tax various business activities as well. Although not widely used, these taxes pose considerable policy and political problems for local governments.

Local-Option Income and Wage Taxes

In the wake of the tax revolts and resulting property tax limitations, the local-option income tax is often considered an alternative source of revenue for local governments. Indeed, after the 1986 Federal Tax Reform Act, many people thought that local-option income taxes would become an important source of local government revenue. These taxes, unlike sales taxes, remained deductible from federal taxable income.

The revenue-raising potential of taxing personal income never materialized. The percentage of total revenue collected from local-option income taxes barely changed over the past several decades. In 1997, local governments in the United States raised only $14 billion from taxing personal income (U.S. Census Bureau 1998). Local-option income taxes accounted for about 1.5 percent of total local government revenue and 4 percent of total local government tax revenue in 1997.

The relatively small amount of revenue raised by local-option income taxes is in part attributable to the fact that few states authorize their use. Only 15 states allow local governments to tax some form of personal income.[1] In two of the states (Arkansas and Georgia), despite having the authority, no local governments have opted to tax income. And only two states—Pennsylvania and Ohio—use local-option income taxes on a large scale. In 1998, Pennsylvania and Ohio collected $2.8 billion and $2.2 billion, respectively, in personal income taxes (U.S. Census Bureau 2000). Together, those two states collected more than one-third of all local personal income taxes in the United States in 1998. In 2000, 543 municipalities in Ohio and 2,879 municipalities in Pennsylvania taxed income (Schmarr and Spretnak 2000).

The states vary in their authorization of local-option income taxes, with some granting authority to all local governments and some allowing only designated jurisdictions to impose the tax. In contrast to the broad local authority granted in Ohio and Pennsylvania, New York only authorizes two cities to tax income. Four states (Kentucky, Iowa, Pennsylvania, and Ohio) also allow school districts to tax income.

Although local governments outside of Pennsylvania and Ohio have not relied heavily on the local-option income tax, the tax has played an important role in financing large cities. In 1990, the latest year for which data are available, personal income taxes accounted for 22 percent of total tax revenue for cities with populations over 300,000 (U.S. Census Bureau 1992). This relatively high yield was achieved despite the fact that only 13 of the 57 cities with populations of 300,000 or more levied the tax.

Local-option income taxes primarily take one of two forms—a wage (or payroll) tax or a general income tax (also known as a piggyback tax). Wage taxes are the most common form of taxing personal income. In 1998, at least 3,643 local governments in nine states imposed a tax on wages earned in their jurisdictions.[2] These taxes, imposed as a flat percentage of earnings or wages, do not apply to unearned income, such as dividends, interest, and capital gains. Generally, no deductions or exemptions apply to the amount subject to tax.

Under most wage tax systems, the localities where individuals reside or work levy taxes. Local governments can, but are usually not required to, give credit for taxes paid to localities of employment. In most states, the tax is administered by the local government imposing the levy.

The piggyback tax is levied by local governments in Iowa and Maryland, usually at a low flat rate, on all residents' income. Thus, the piggyback tax is imposed on a much greater base than wage taxes. The state collects the bulk of the tax through withholdings, and residents pay the remainder when they file their state income tax returns. The state then remits the local portion of the income tax to the local government serving the taxpayer's residential area. The state performs all the administrative functions of the tax.

Policy Issues of Taxing Income and Wages

Income and wage taxes present different policy issues for lawmakers and local policy leaders. Like other taxation decisions, taxing income and wages has both benefits and costs.

VISIBILITY AND ACCOUNTABILITY

Theoretically, both piggyback and wage taxes are attractive tax policy choices because they are highly visible. For wage earners, employers withhold both types of income taxes. Thus, the taxpayer can see, on a weekly or biweekly basis, how much tax is being paid to support local government services.

As noted in chapter 3, visibility allows taxpayers to determine how much money they are spending on government. Such visibility gives citizens the incentive to hold elected officials accountable for how their money is being spent, a hallmark of good government. Visibility also prevents governments from hiding tax burdens from citizens.

ECONOMIC EFFICIENCY

While both wage and piggyback taxes earn high marks for visibility, they fare differently in terms of economic efficiency. Many economists and public finance experts regard the piggyback tax as an efficient means of raising revenue (see, for example, Bird 1993). Indeed, since only residents pay piggyback local income taxes, the tax conforms to the benefits principle of taxation. It cannot easily be exported to nonresidents. Thus, only residents who receive the public services provided by the local government are responsible for paying the tax.

The piggyback tax places few administrative burdens or costs on local governments. As noted, the tax is collected as part of the state income tax and is remitted by the state to the locality of residence. The state bears all audit and collection responsibilities for the tax. In this regard, most observers have opined that the piggyback tax presents few administrative difficulties for local governments (Liner 1992).

The local-option income tax also does not place serious compliance burdens on individual taxpayers (Liner 1992). Taxpayers pay the tax as part of their compliance with state income tax laws. There are no additional reporting requirements or forms to file beyond those required for state personal income taxes.

Wage taxes, however, are widely viewed as inefficient methods for collecting revenue. Because wage taxes do not conform to state income tax laws, local governments must administer and enforce wage tax laws, making the tax much more expensive to administer. In addition to administering the tax, local governments must perform all audit and collection activities. Thus, in wage tax jurisdictions, both the compliance and administrative costs are higher than those for states levying a piggyback tax.

Moreover, in some wage-tax states, particularly Ohio, the local tax is not uniform across the state. This variance creates problems for employers with workers in more than one locality. Each municipality can define taxable wages, establish filing deadlines for employers, and determine whether to offer credits and the amount. Critics have called Ohio's local wage tax system unnecessarily complex (Schmarr and Spretnak 2000).[3]

The payroll tax also places compliance burdens on individual employees. Each municipality must administer its own tax, and the employee must file returns in the place of residency. This requirement means employees must file three income tax returns (federal, state, and local) each year. All local-option income taxes that do not conform to the state tax base and to state filing requirements will be more expensive for both governments and taxpayers (Schmarr and Spretnak 2000).

REVENUE GROWTH AND DIVERSIFICATION

Both wage and piggyback taxes bring a measure of diversity to the local tax system. As noted in chapter 3, tax diversity adds stability and reliability to the system. Income tax revenue grows more quickly than either local-option sales or property tax revenue. A 10 percent increase in income will yield a greater than 10 percent increase in income tax revenue. This revenue-producing potential greatly benefits local governments during times of strong economic growth. It also appeals to government leaders, because they realize that tax revenue increases without them having to take the political risks that would accompany a raise in rates. During times of economic slowdown, however, the opposite is true. Income tax revenue tends to fall more precipitously than other types of tax revenue during an economic downturn.

Diverse revenue sources allow localities to maintain more control over their financial systems.[4] This control is particularly important today, because local governments have limited options for taxing property and consumption.

FAIRNESS

Questions of fairness are among the most difficult to answer when it comes to tax policy choices. The generally accepted view is that fairness requires governments to minimize their use of taxes that burden poorer residents more than wealthier residents. The limitations posed by inter-jurisdictional competition generally prevent local governments from imposing progressive taxes that redistribute wealth from wealthier to poorer segments of society.

Generally, local income taxes (specifically, piggyback taxes) can increase the progressivity of the tax system. A piggyback local-option income tax system would impose greater burdens on higher-income taxpayers than on lower-income taxpayers. Essentially, the tax would have the same degree of progressivity as the state income tax. (Most state income taxes are considered mildly progressive; see, for example, Brunori 2001e.) Overall, because of heavy reliance on consumption taxes, local tax systems tend to be regressive. The local-option income tax, if tied to the state system, would bring a measure of progressivity to local finance (see, for example, Strauss 1995).

State and local political leaders and policymakers are well aware of the limits on redistributing wealth at the local level. Arguably, so few states impose the piggyback income tax because of its progressivity. Most states that allow their localities to tax income limit the tax to earned income—a much more regressive alternative.

Unlike piggyback taxes, local-option wage taxes pose serious equity issues. First, these taxes are generally viewed as regressive, because lower-income residents are likely to earn most of their income from taxable wages, while wealthier residents receive a far larger percentage of their income from nonwage sources not subject to tax (Liner 1992; Wallace and Edwards 1999). In addition, payroll tax systems do not allow for exemptions or deductions, which would provide relief to the poorest employees.

The equity issues do not end with wealthy citizens bearing less of the burden of paying for government. Tax systems should be horizontally equitable, with similarly situated taxpayers taxed similarly (Reese 1980). In a wage-tax system, even wealthy citizens who earn most or all of their income from wages are treated unfairly because payroll taxes are not horizontally equitable. Residents who earn all of their income from wages are taxed, while residents who earn all of their income from dividends, interest, or capital gains are not taxed. Such dissimilar treatment causes the public to distrust the tax system as well as government in general (Brunori 2001e).

FISCAL DISPARITIES

Another problem with local-option income taxes is that they increase fiscal disparities between local jurisdictions. As explained in chapter 5, one of the problems with property taxes is that they lead to fiscal disparities, particularly with respect to education finance. The use of income taxes in lieu of property taxes, once thought a way to potentially offset revenue shortfalls, is not a solution. By some measures, tax-base disparities are actually larger under local income and sales tax than under property taxes (Bowman and Mikesell 1978a; McGuire 2001). The disparities are evident for both wage and piggyback taxes, because local jurisdictions vary in their populations of wealthy residents and levels of employment.

TAXING COMMUTERS OR EXPORTING TAX BURDENS

One advantage of a local payroll tax is that nonresident commuters are forced to bear a share of the costs of local government. Ladd and Yinger (1989) find that commuters increase a local government's costs, particularly in the areas of police and fire protection. Nonresident visitors, particularly commuters, consume public services such as transportation, public safety, and parks. A payroll tax collected by employment locality ensures that commuters are paying for at least some of the services they receive.

Taxing commuters, however, also provides the opportunity to export tax burdens. Tax exporting in this context occurs when local governments impose taxes on commuters in excess of the costs of services consumed by the commuters. Payroll taxes can be exported to nonresidents far more effectively than property or sales taxes (Ladd and Yinger 1989). The ability to export tax burdens counters the general bias against income taxes.

INTERGOVERNMENTAL ISSUES

Intergovernmental issues that arise when local governments attempt to tax income prevent the tax from being used more widely. Local-option income taxes generally reduce states' income tax flexibility. Broadening or narrowing the tax base and increasing or reducing rates become more difficult for the states if local governments also rely on the tax.

Multiple levels of government taxing the same base hurts the efficiency and effectiveness of a tax. When two levels of government tax the same base, the combined tax rate tends to be inefficiently large (Sobel 1997). When one level of government chooses to levy a tax, it has no incentive to take the other government's tax rate into account. The result can be relatively high combined state and local income tax rates. In New York, for example, the combined highest New York City and New York State tax rate in 2000 was 10.4 percent. The rate was higher than the national average and nearly double the average maximum rate imposed by states that did not allow local-option income taxes.

While reduced flexibility is a concern, state and local policymakers often overlook one of the benefits of local-option income taxes. Citizens who itemize their federal tax returns can deduct state and local income taxes from federal taxable income. Federal deductibility shifts some of the costs of paying for local services to the federal government—and to other taxpayers. Thus, local income taxes should, in theory, have the same political appeal as any exportable tax.

POLITICAL BIAS

Political bias against the tax is one of the primary reasons reliance on local-option income taxes is unlikely to increase. This bias is well documented at the state level (Beamer 2000, Brunori 2001e). When states need to raise additional revenue, they are far more likely to increase sales and use taxes through either base broadening or rate hikes than through increases in personal income taxes (see, for example, Brunori 2001e). Conversely, when states have the opportunity to reduce tax burdens, they are far more likely to cut personal income taxes through additional exemptions and deductions or rate decreases than they are to cut the more regressive consumption taxes.

This bias carries over to local income taxes for several reasons: Many political leaders and academics believe that income taxation deters economic growth. The perception is that relatively higher income tax burdens place state and local governments at a competitive disadvantage relative to jurisdictions with lower income tax burdens. Income taxes are thought to hamper efforts to attract homeowners and businesses to the jurisdiction and to retain them once they get there.

Although the research is mixed, many studies have found that local-option income taxes do deter economic development.[5] Grieson (1980) and Stull and Stull (1991), for example, find that commuter taxes had a negative impact on both employment levels and housing values. Nechyba (1997) finds that mobility within metropolitan areas explains why local governments do not tax income. Moreover, one study found evidence that a 1977 wage tax increase in Philadelphia led directly to the loss of between 100,000 and 165,000 jobs (Crapo 2001). In addition, extensive anecdotal evidence has created a powerful perception that local governments are better off without such taxes. This perception has helped fuel the political bias against the income tax.

As stated in chapter 3, political leaders are primarily concerned with economic growth and job creation. This focus creates a strong bias against policies that hinder—or give the perception of hindering—those goals. The personal income tax has long been thought to have a detrimental effect on the economy. Other levies, such as those on consumption or property, have never suffered from this perception. Thus, when faced with the choice of raising revenue through income or other types of taxes, legislators usually opt for the latter.

Finally, legislators may intentionally decide to reduce income tax burdens knowing full well that the wealthier segments of society will benefit most, because wealthier taxpayers are more likely than poorer taxpayers to vote—and to contribute to political campaigns (see, for example, Brunori 2001e). While difficult to prove, such a claim suggests that legislators avoid raising income taxes for this reason.

Outlook

Relatively few local governments outside Ohio and Pennsylvania impose local-option income taxes. The political bias against such taxes and the competition between local governments create almost insurmountable obstacles to the growth of the tax. Even in the largest cities, where local-option income taxes once dominated local finance, the tax may be in jeopardy. Strauss and Nakamura (1999), after studying urban migration patterns in the 1990s, found that residents leaving cities had much higher incomes than those migrating to cities. If such patterns persist, the local-option income tax may cease to be an important source of revenue in the nation's largest cities.

Local-Option Business Taxes

In addition to taxing personal income, 15 states allow local governments to tax business entities and activities.[6] Such local-option business taxes take various forms, including gross receipts taxes, net income or profits taxes, payroll taxes, license taxes, and business personal property taxes. These taxes are all levied apart from the traditional taxes on real property.

Most public finance experts believe business taxes deter economic development. They also spur competition between local governments vying for businesses to locate or to remain in their districts.

Despite the widespread disapproval, 14 states still authorize local governments to impose business taxes. Taxing businesses holds a certain political appeal. Business tax burdens can often be exported to nonresidents—a strategy favored by politicians. Because citizens often separate business entities from their owners, customers, and employees, the public may view business taxes as "victimless" (Youngman 1999c). Yet owners, customers, and employees are the ones who ultimately bear the tax burden.

The small number of state governments that allow local business taxation reflects the widespread agreement among policymakers and public finance experts that such taxes are not an effective or efficient source of revenue. In most of the 14 states allowing the local taxation of business interests, various groups continue to lobby for their repeal (Brunori 2001e). The reason for the relatively low usage is the belief that business taxation deters economic growth and hurts the community's competitiveness. Differences in inter-local tax burdens also affect business location decisions (Wayslenko 1986).

The four main types of local-option business taxes are local-option business income taxes, gross receipts/license taxes, business personal property taxes, and payroll taxes.

Local-Option Business Income Taxes

In the United States, eight states authorize local governments to impose taxes on corporate income.[7] In 1997, local governments raised $3 billion from corporate income taxes (U.S. Census Bureau 1998). The rates, tax base, and filing requirements differ from those for states and the federal government, making local corporate income taxes among the most controversial of all local taxes. In jurisdictions with the tax, corporate taxpayers must calculate local income tax liabilities separately. This added burden greatly increases the costs of compliance. Moreover, because the tax does not comply with state or federal law, the local governments must independently administer the tax.

Local-option corporate income taxes present other serious compliance and administrative problems for taxpayers and the government. Taxpayers must determine the amount of income attributable to the local jurisdiction imposing the tax. Such apportionment and allocation issues are very difficult at the state level and are greatly magnified when dealing with local income taxes. Because many corporations conduct business in several jurisdictions, taxpayers and tax collectors alike have difficulty determining how much income is taxable in a particular jurisdiction. Localities using the tax often have different tax bases, tax rates, and filing requirements. State-imposed uniformity standards on local-option corporate income taxes can mitigate this problem, but such uniformity requirements are rare.

A more significant problem for policymakers is that local corporate income taxes spur competition among localities. Local political leaders understand that corporate tax burdens influence firms' location decisions. As a result, cities often offer tax reductions to lure firms to an area or to convince them to remain in the city. Such competition is consistent with both the imperative to spur economic wealth and the concept that local governments cannot effectively tax business income in a federalist system.

Gross Receipts/License Taxes

In four states,[8] local governments are authorized to impose business taxes based on a firm's gross receipts (National Conference of State Legislatures 1997a). For economic development purposes, states commonly vary rates by type of business. Gross receipts taxes typically do not take profitability into account. Such laws present startup businesses and established companies encountering market difficulties with particular hardships.

The administrative and compliance costs associated with gross receipts taxes are relatively high, especially for businesses operating in multiple jurisdictions. Such businesses incur multiple accounting and compliance costs in determining the gross receipts attributable to each jurisdiction. Moreover, many jurisdictions within the same state have differing tax rates, tax bases, and reporting requirements. Complying with gross receipts taxes in multiple jurisdictions adds significantly to the costs.

The administrative costs for the government are also relatively high. Local governments must track and assess the gross receipts that arise from multijurisdictional transactions. State-mandated uniformity can reduce administrative costs, but such uniformity provisions are rare.

Gross receipts taxes also fuel interjurisdictional competition. Differences in gross receipts tax burdens can affect business location decisions. This competition creates pressure on local governments to reduce tax rates and offer incentive packages to retain or lure new business. Such competition continually shrinks the gross receipts tax base.

Business Personal Property Taxes

Although they are usually administered as part of the general property tax system, many local governments impose property tax levies on business personal property. Indeed, 44 states provide for taxation of depreciable assets of business, and 16 states subject business inventory to a property tax (Papke 2000). Business property tax rates vary widely. In Indiana, for example, 2,143 local governments impose effective rates from 1.5 to 5.4 percent (Papke 2000).

Despite the widespread use of personal property taxes, many economists and political leaders view the taxes as an inefficient way to raise revenue. And, in almost every state, they continually try to repeal all or part of the tax on business personal property.

Papke (2000, 671) describes the problems such taxation poses:

> It is administratively difficult to obtain accurate assessment of the value of machinery, equipment, and inventories.
>
> Inventories, in particular, are difficult, if not impossible to assess properly. They vary from raw materials to goods in process to finished products, are mobile (i.e., they can be moved from one jurisdiction to another within a taxable period), and have different turnover rates. As a consequence of administrative deficiencies, business personality is frequently assessed by negotiation between taxpayer and assessor resulting in unequal application among jurisdictions and between taxpayers within the same jurisdiction. The tax on business personalty is a tax on the employment of capital. Other things equal, if factor proportions are variable, imposition of the tax leads to a substitution of tax-free factors for the taxed inputs, the extent depending upon the supply elasticities of the various factors and the production function. Taxes on machinery, equipment, tools, and inventories may impede capital investment, particularly in industries making frequent changes in product development and design. The tax bears little or no relationship to the scale and volume of business output or to the costs or value of government services provided.

Such deficiencies have even been identified by scholars and public finance experts who see virtues in taxing tangible personal property. Cornia and Wheeler (1999) note that personal property taxes are difficult and expensive to administer and enforce and that they create horizontal inequities between firms with significant amounts of tangible assets and firms with few such assets.[9]

Significant anecdotal evidence suggests that imposing personal property taxes deters economic development. While scant scholarly evidence exists to support such a view, political leaders across the United States tailor their policies to fit these perceived views. The real and perceived problems with the tax have led many leading economists to argue that the tax should be abandoned as a source of revenue for local governments (see, for example, Papke 2000).

Payroll Taxes

Six states authorize local governments to tax businesses on the basis of payroll in their jurisdiction.[10] The tax is imposed on the employer and is usually a percentage of total payroll within the city or county imposing the tax. In that regard, the tax is distinguishable from payroll or wage taxes, which are imposed on the employee. In two states—Illinois and

Washington—the tax is imposed as a flat per employee fee, commonly known as a head tax.

Payroll taxes, by some accounts, present less administrative and compliance burdens on taxpayers and governments than other types of business taxes (Crapo 2001). But small businesses and out-of-state businesses conducting limited operations within the boundaries of the city or county that imposes the tax face greater burdens.

Despite the relatively low administrative and compliance burdens, business widely criticizes payroll taxes as deterring economic development. Such taxes fall heavily on labor-intensive businesses, and they result in higher employee compensation costs. Such costs affect business location decisions—a fact that, in turn, can lead local governments to lower payroll taxes or offer incentives to retain or attract business. Indeed, Crapo (2001) found that payroll taxes hurt job creation and economic development. Business lobbyists also criticize payroll taxes for imposing burdens on businesses that may be losing money. Startup businesses and firms in segments of the economy susceptible to economic downturn are particularly vulnerable in a system that imposes taxes without regard to income.

Outlook for Business Taxes

Many scholars and policymakers agree that local-option business taxes are neither a practical nor a theoretically sound way to raise revenue for local governments. Indeed, one noted scholar asserts that "There is little case for allowing local governments a free hand in taxing business, whether such taxes take the form of the nonresident property tax, corporate income tax, or taxes on gross sales, or business activity" (Bird 1993, 216).

Conclusion

Income and business taxes are not likely to play a more important role in financing local government (see Sheffrin 1998). Rather, the percentage of revenue raised from income and business taxes will likely continue to decline (see Pogue 1998). Both income and business taxes impose burdens on mobile bases, and those bases can and will be moved. Political leaders perceive both income and business taxes as detrimental to economic development. This perception alone makes increased reliance on the income and business taxes unlikely.

These taxes are incapable of substituting for local property taxes. The evidence also suggests that moving toward greater reliance on income taxes at the expense of property taxes would place greater burdens on individuals (Strauss 2001). Many policymakers would find this outcome politically unpalatable.

NOTES

1. The states that allow local-option income taxes are Alabama, Arkansas, Colorado, Delaware, Georgia, Indiana, Iowa, Kentucky, Maryland, Michigan, Missouri, New York, Ohio, Pennsylvania, and Washington.

2. The states with localities imposing wage taxes are Alabama, Delaware, Indiana, Kentucky, Michigan, Missouri, New York, Ohio, and Pennsylvania. In addition, Colorado and Washington allow local governments to impose head taxes, which are levied at a flat rate per employee.

3. Compared with Ohio, Pennsylvania relies more heavily on payroll taxes and requires much more uniformity with respect to rates, the base, filing requirements, and credits (Schmarr and Spretnak 2000).

4. This control is not absolute. Local-option income taxes must be approved by the states. Moreover, in every jurisdiction, the authority to set rates is limited by state statute or voter approval requirements.

5. Tuerck et al. (2001) argue that local-option income taxes reduce employment. Adler, Cook, and Parrott (2002) argue that such taxes *do not* reduce employment.

6. Arkansas, California, Illinois, Kentucky, Michigan, Missouri, New Jersey, New York, Ohio, Oregon, Pennsylvania, Tennessee, Virginia, Washington, and West Virginia allow local-option business taxes. Local governments in Arkansas have not opted to impose such taxes.

7. Kentucky, Missouri, Michigan, New York, Ohio, Oregon, Tennessee, and West Virginia allow some local governments to tax corporate income.

8. Georgia, Pennsylvania, Virginia, and Washington allow local governments to impose gross receipts/license taxes.

9. Cornia and Wheeler (1999) argue that the tax on personal property can provide a stable source of revenue for local governments.

10. California, Illinois, Missouri, New Jersey, Oregon, and Washington allow local governments to impose payroll taxes on businesses.

8

Nontax Revenue Options

Whenever possible, local public services should be charged for.

—Richard Bird, 1993

The last two chapters addressed the various non-property-tax alternatives available to local governments. Taxes are not the only sources of revenue for local governments. Local governments in the United States raise most of their total revenue from nontax sources, a fact little understood by even the most informed citizens. These nontax revenue sources became increasingly important to local governments over the course of the 1990s. In 1992, local governments raised approximately $420 billion from nontax sources—about 62 percent of their total revenue. By 1999, local governments raised approximately $637 billion in nontax revenue—66 percent of their total revenue (U.S. Census Bureau 2000).

Local governments have three primary sources of nontax revenue: intergovernmental aid (primarily from the states), user fees and charges, and the operation of utilities. Each of these sources presents unique issues for local government finance.

Intergovernmental Aid

Transfers of money from state, and to a much lesser extent federal, governments constitute the largest single source of nontax revenue for local governments. In 1999, local governments received approximately $296 billion from the states, about 31 percent of their total revenue. In the same year, local governments received an additional $31 billion from the federal government, just under 3 percent of total revenue. The combined federal and state intergovernmental aid surpassed the aggregate amount of total own-source taxes ($315 billion) raised by local governments in that same year (U.S. Census Bureau 2000). Intergovernmental state aid has steadily increased both in terms of actual dollars and as a percentage of total local government revenue. In 1992, state aid to local governments totaled approximately $195 billion, or about 30 percent of total local government revenue (U.S. Census Bureau 1993).

The increase in the amount of state aid to local governments primarily reflects the increased centralization of public education finance. As explained in chapter 5, state governments today finance most elementary and secondary schools, expenses once paid almost exclusively by localities. Of the $296 billion transferred from state to local governments in 1999, $172 billion, or 58 percent, directly funded public elementary and secondary education (U.S. Census Bureau 2000).

Although state intergovernmental aid has steadily increased, federal aid to local governments has decreased as a percentage of total revenue. In 1978, federal aid to local governments accounted for 10 percent of total local revenue, nearly three times the percentage raised in 1999 (U.S. Census Bureau 2000).

The federal government originally targeted local aid to large cities contending with declining populations, an eroding tax base, and increased public service demands. In 1977, large cities received 44 percent of their total revenue directly from the federal government.[1] Federal aid to large cities constituted the largest percentage of aid to local governments. Between 1981 and 1993, federal aid to cities fell 66 percent in real dollars (Paget 1998). County governments suffered similar cuts. Between 1980 and 1986, the federal government cut aid to counties by 73 percent (Rymarowicz and Zimmerman 1988). The decline in federal aid to local governments is largely attributable to a change in federal policy on intergovernmental aid and fiscal federalism.

Policy Justifications for Intergovernmental Aid

State aid to local governments—the most significant type of intergovernmental aid— helps local governments manage limitations on their ability to raise own-source revenue. Property tax limitations, along with inherent limitations on the ability to collect other types of taxes, have put enormous pressure on local governments. State government aid has allowed local governments to continue operating despite the varied limitations on their taxing authority. States have imposed most tax limitations. State intergovernmental aid helps compensate local governments for the lost revenue.

In this regard, state aid is recognition that local governments are incapable of funding government services through their own tax systems, at least as they are now structured. The public's demands for services exceed the local governments' means of paying for such services. Local government inability to cover the costs of services is tied directly to the limitations placed on the property tax, particularly rate and assessment limitations. But such limitations are, at least in the foreseeable future, a legal and political reality.

Intergovernmental aid also helps localities finance services that benefit residents beyond their borders. Large cities, for example, provide services that benefit commuters, tourists, and other nonresidents. Local residents are forced to pay for the services provided to nonresidents. As the previous two chapters document, some local governments collect taxes from nonresidents (through payroll, sales, and property taxes). But these tax sources, when available, often cannot cover the marginal costs of providing the services to nonresidents. In such instances, state aid helps compensate local governments for the costs of providing benefits to people and business outside their jurisdiction.

Perhaps the most controversial reason for the increase in intergovernmental aid is the attempt to address fiscal inequalities within states. As explained in chapter 5, wealthier localities collect more taxes and can spend more on basic public services than poorer communities. Such fiscal disparities have sparked efforts to "equalize" the financing of certain public services, particularly public education.

State governments have tried to equalize local government finances in several ways. Some state governments have simply taken responsibility for paying for all, or almost all, of a particular local government service. In 1994, for example, Michigan assumed responsibility for financing elementary and secondary education in the state, so that local governments now have virtually no role in financing public education in Michigan. To finance the equalization of school spending among different localities, Michigan increased statewide sales taxes.

Vermont and New Hampshire adopted statewide property taxes to try to equalize school funding. Such taxes redistribute property tax revenue from wealthier to poorer communities. Statewide property taxes are among the most politically controversial methods of fiscal equalization. The property tax provides a local source of revenue, but the tax engenders even more opposition when used to redistribute wealth.

The actual determination of state aid is made by the legislature, usually based on a statutory formula. Most states provide funding to all school districts. The funding levels are usually determined by tax capacity and student population and are aimed at providing additional revenue to poorer school districts.

Problems with Intergovernmental Aid

Unreliability

One of the most significant problems with the increased reliance on intergovernmental aid is that such aid can be unreliable. State governments have been forced to increase aid to local governments during the property tax revolts and as part of school funding equalization. But in most cases, states have no minimum funding requirements. And there are few guarantees that funding will even continue. Intergovernmental aid is appropriated at the discretion of the state legislature. The monies to be handed over to the local governments are not determined or controlled by the people on whose behalf they will be spent.

The inability of local governments to rely on state aid poses particular problems during times of economic downturn (Brunori 2001d). When states face serious budget crises, as they did in the early 1980s, early 1990s, and in 2001–02, states typically cut aid to local governments before reducing other expenditures (Sokolow 1998). During the 2001–02 state budget crisis, 32 states reduced aid to local governments, cuts that together amounted to an estimated $15 billion. In 2002, North Carolina alone reduced direct aid to local governments by $330 million. The decision to reduce aid to North Carolina cities and counties was a direct result of the state's budget deficit of $1 billion. The budget cuts caused local governments to ask the North Carolina legislature for authority to impose various new taxes and fees, including an additional half-cent increase in the local-option sales tax.

The problems of relying on a legislature with shifting priorities occur not only during times of recession. When states are running large budget surpluses—as was the norm during the mid- and late 1990s—legislators are more apt to cut taxes or to increase state spending than to increase intergovernmental aid. Cutting taxes or financing state projects creates more political cachet than does increasing local government aid. Mayors, city managers, and county executives will incur the wrath of residents if public services are not adequately provided because of a lack of funding. Those same political leaders will reap the benefits if the citizenry is satisfied with the mix of services and taxes. State legislators, however, have little to gain from ensuring that local government aid is maintained at levels deemed acceptable to local residents. State legislators may direct funds to other public services, despite the need of the local governments.

One of the most significant problems associated with relying on state aid is that local governments can become dependent on the fortunes of the state budget. This reliance is particularly problematic when states face budget deficits. During times of recession, state tax revenue declines, leaving state political leaders with essentially three policy choices: They can raise taxes, cut public services, or combine tax increases with service reductions.

As a result, local governments are often forced to lobby for additional resources. State associations of municipalities and counties routinely take their case to the legislature and argue for more funding. The problem for the cities and counties, however, is that many other organizations and interests are also lobbying for more support. As Sokolow (2000, 104) notes, "In a centralized fiscal environment, local governments are merely another set of competitors for scarce state budget dollars."

But intergovernmental aid distributed according to the priorities set by effective lobbying efforts is not necessarily the most efficient way to finance government. Local governments will lobby for as much revenue as possible, regardless of need (Berman 2000). Local governments will lobby for aid to pay for nonessential projects rather than let state money flow to neighboring jurisdictions (Levine and Posner 1981). Moreover, once the local government begins receiving intergovernmental aid for specific programs, local agencies tend to protect these programs, and the state aid they receive, even at the expense of locally funded programs (Levine and Posner 1981).

More significantly, increased state aid must be paid for with additional state revenue. Increased state aid is accompanied by increased state tax burdens (Sokolow 1998). The public and many political leaders seemingly do not understand the connection between state aid and state tax burdens. Residents certainly appreciate lower local tax burdens. They may not realize, however, that state tax burdens have increased to maintain a satisfactory level of local public services.

State aid places local governments in a difficult position. No local public leader will turn down funding from the state, especially during times of economic slowdown. Some evidence suggests that following the tax revolts, local politicians preferred to ask for more aid rather than to ask for increased taxing power (Sokolow 1998).

LESS AUTONOMY

When states grant funding to, or assume financing of, services traditionally performed by local governments, local governments lose a measure of autonomy. Funding from higher levels of government inevitably comes with "strings attached." State legislators appropriating revenue take an interest in how the money will be spent, and research shows that states routinely impose restrictions on how state aid should be spent (see, for example, Nice and Fredericksen 1998, 156, and references therein). The state legislatures inevitably exert expanded influence over traditionally local matters. Intergovernmental aid results in a loss of political autonomy by the recipient of such aid.

EFFICIENCY

Intergovernmental aid not only diminishes political autonomy but also erodes economic efficiency. Centralization clearly reduces the economic benefits of intergovernmental competition (Holcombe 1998). In addition, intergovernmental aid leads to "fiscal illusions," because recipients of local public services do not realize the true costs of those services. As a result, demand for such services increases, resulting in a larger-than-optimal public sector (Oates 1979).

The level of funding and the conditions placed on that funding may result in public services that do not match the preferences of the people who live in the locality. This mismatch creates inefficiency. In an influential report, the National Conference of State Legislators notes:

> The primary disadvantage of centralization is loss of local control and accountability. Especially in geographically large states—which can encompass politically diverse urban, suburban, and rural areas—centralization increases the likelihood that some residents will be taxed for services they do not want or need. Proponents

of decentralization argue that local residents are best suited to decide the service and tax levels that suit their needs (1997b, 5).

Consequences for Local Tax Policy

The rise and dominance of state intergovernmental aid has hurt local governments' tax autonomy. Localities using state aid to finance government services have difficulty mustering public or political support for local taxes. Even if fundamental public services are in need of additional revenue, local political leaders will tend to look to the state rather than to own-source revenue. The existence of state aid reinforces the logic for a politician to look for state aid to fund public services rather than take the politically risky option of advocating greater tax burdens on his or her constituents.

Intergovernmental aid further reduces the ability of local governments to raise tax revenue. The inability to raise sufficient tax revenue has the effect of forcing local governments to rely even more heavily on intergovernmental aid.

User Fees and Charges

User fees and charges are the second most significant source of nontax revenue for local governments after intergovernmental aid. Virtually every local government in the United States attaches user fees and charges to some services, such as parks and recreation, sanitation, sewage, hospital, parking, and airport services. Local governments also impose business license fees, professional license fees, and automobile registration fees.[2]

Over the past quarter-century—since the onset of the tax revolts—state and local governments have increasingly relied on user fees and charges to fund public services. Local governments raised in aggregate $195 billion, or 20 percent of their total revenue, from user fees and charges in 1999, compared with $132 billion, or 12 percent of total revenue, in 1992. This rapid growth largely reflects limitations placed on localities' ability to increase other revenue sources, particularly the property tax (O'Sullivan 2000; Sexton, Sheffrin, and O'Sullivan 1999; Shadbegian 1998). In Colorado, after significant property tax limitations, cities and towns tried to shift their revenue reliance from property taxes to user fees as much as possible (Brown 2000). As a result, Colorado localities experienced tremendous growth in user fee revenue.

Local governments do not all rely on user fees and charges to the same extent. Some local governments tend to rely heavily on user charges, employing fees for many services, while other local governments use them much more selectively (Downing 1992). California, for example, relies heavily on user charges. In the wake of Proposition 13, California cities turned increasingly to user fees and charges—such as new building/developer fees, real estate transfer fees, new or higher business license fees, utility user fees, sewer charges, and increased park and recreation fees—to offset lost property tax revenue. From 1978 to 1993, current service charges for all California cities combined increased 193 percent, from 25 percent of city revenue to 40 percent of city revenue. Among nonenterprise special districts (e.g., parks, libraries, police, and fire protection districts), fees increased from 7 percent of revenue in 1978 to 38 percent in 1990 (Sexton and Sheffrin 1995).

In addition to the traditional charges described here, local governments have developed new fees to boost revenue. Two common types of new charges used by local governments are development fees and exactions, payments made by developers for the right to proceed with a project.[3] Such fees are used to support new government services that will be needed once the development is complete, such as water, sewage, roads, parks, and schools. The conventional thinking is that new residents ultimately bear those fees in the form of higher housing and building costs. In that sense, these fees are logically viewed as user fees for new development (Dresch and Sheffrin 1997).

Other financing techniques that have been greatly expanded since Proposition 13 include the establishment of special assessment districts, known in California as Mello-Roos community facilities districts. Within such districts, local governments can collect per parcel fees to pay for local improvements. Special assessment fees may be used to pay for any public improvement of direct benefit to the property, such as flood control, drainage, and street lighting.

Special assessment fees increased 372 percent between 1983 and 1993, from $64.4 million to $304.1 million (Sexton and Sheffrin 1995). Few limitations apply to the use of these financing mechanisms, which are being used to finance police and fire protection, library services, park and recreation services, and flood and storm services as well as facilities such as streets, water, sewer and drainage construction, parks, schools, libraries, jails, and administrative facilities. In California, Mello-Roos financings totaled nearly $1 billion by 1990 (Sexton and Sheffrin 1995).

The increased use of fees and charges reflects a desire on the part of local political entities to retain control over their finances. User fees and charges are generally not subject to the legal constraints imposed on property and other taxes. It should be noted that because user fees and charges are not subject to most tax limitations, they are prone to criticism by anti-tax advocates.

Policy Reasons for Imposing Charges

Along with the property tax, user fees and charges are widely regarded as an effective means of raising local revenue. User fees and charges do not present many of the same problems as taxes. They have limited effects on redistribution of wealth and distortion of the markets. For these reasons, many leading economists and public finance experts endorse their use (see, for example, Bird 1993; Break 1993; Downing 1999; Gramlich 1993; McKinnon and Nechyba 1997; Oates 1993; Wassmer 1998).

ECONOMIC EFFICIENCY
The primary justification for user fees and charges is that they are among the most efficient means of financing local government services (Bland 1997; Downing 1999; Wassmer 1998). As noted in chapter 3, benefit taxes are an efficient, effective way of paying for local public services. User fees and charges are often considered the truest form of a benefits tax. From an economic efficiency standpoint, user fees and charges "take the benefits received theory of taxation to its logical conclusion" (Bierhanzl and Downing 1998, 175). Only those who use the public service pay the fee or charge. Individuals who prefer not to receive or use the particular service do not incur additional costs (Batt 1993).

User fees allow local governments to avoid oversupplying services and unnecessarily expanding the public sector. Moreover, user fees and charges reduce the occurrence of tax exporting and fiscal illusion that causes excess demand for public services (Bierhanzl and Downing 1998). User fees are virtually impossible to export to nonbeneficiaries of the services provided.[4]

User fees and charges are also attractive because they may reduce firm and individual migration. User fees should reflect the true marginal cost of public services. If individuals and firms receive the public services they desire at a cost they are willing to pay, they will have less incentive to search for a more optimal service/tax mix. This efficiency provides a clear advantage for using charges as opposed to virtually any type of general tax.

For these reasons, a local finance system based on user fees has long been considered ideal from an efficiency standpoint. The economic efficiencies and the ability to control some portion of their tax burden have translated into broad public support for user fees and charges. Public acceptance, in turn, ensures the support of political leaders.

DIVERSIFICATION OF REVENUE SOURCES
With property taxes under intense pressure, user fees and charges allow local governments to diversify their revenue base. As noted in chapter 3, sound tax systems need a diverse base to ensure stability. State and local finance systems have traditionally relied upon income, sales, and property taxes to fund government. In light of the limitations on other tax sources, user fees have come to play a major role in both state and local public finance systems.

LOCAL CONTROL
Because user fees and charges are not generally subject to the legal limitations imposed on other taxes, user fees and charges allow local governments to retain a measure of control over their finances. Local governments generally do not require legislative approval to impose fees and charges. Despite political and market limitations, user fees and charges have helped local governments weather the property tax revolts.

Problems with Imposing Charges

Despite widespread public acceptance and support by most scholars, user fees and charges pose policy problems for local governments.

LIMITATIONS ON REVENUE GROWTH
User fee revenue can increase in one of three ways. First, local governments can raise the nominal rates charged for the particular service. For example, the city or county could raise the fee for access to the public pool from to $5 to $6. Second, user fee revenue will grow if more citizens use and pay for the underlying public services—assuming that the marginal costs of providing that service do not increase. For example, an increase in the number of people using the public pool would, all things being equal, bring in more net revenue. Finally, local governments could increase the number of public services for which fees can

be charged. None of these options is readily available to most local governments.

Local governments cannot raise the price of public services at will. User fees and charges are efficient revenue sources because they reflect the benefits tax principle. User fees that exceed the marginal cost of local public services violate this principle and are likely to depress demand for the service.

The amount that governments can charge for a particular public service is limited (Batt 1993). At some level, citizens will refrain from using a public service when the attached fees are excessive, especially when viable alternatives to the desired government service are available. Because localities cannot impose charges at rates beyond what a person or business would pay, the market limits the amount of revenue local governments can raise from fees.[5]

Local governments generally cannot count on the increased usage of public services to raise user fees and charges. The number of citizens who can access public services at any one time is limited. Moreover, increased usage tends to increase the costs of providing the services.

Finally, the service base upon which fees and charges can be levied generally cannot grow significantly. Local governments cannot realistically charge fees for services that are widely available, such as education, transportation infrastructure, and police and fire protection. This limitation is not unique to local government fees, but is inherent in fees charged by all entities. If a local government cannot control access to the public service, it will have difficulty charging for that service. The problem is that few public services are left that can be subject to discrete fees. Over recent decades, local governments, especially those in states with significant property tax limitations, have imposed fees on just about everything possible. Few public services on which a fee or charge can be imposed remain.

FAIRNESS CONCERNS

Finally, the fairness of using fees and charges to fund public services is questionable. Most residents and policymakers agree that it is patently unfair to charge fees for such essential services as police, fire protection, and other public safety services (see, for example, Batt 1993).

This objection is related to the regressivity of user fees and charges in general. Scholars and public finance practitioners assert that—despite their attributes—user fees and charges are decidedly regressive. That is, people with lower incomes pay a higher percentage of their income in fees and charges than do people with higher incomes.

Outlook for User Fees

Most public finance experts agree that user fees can efficiently finance many local government services (see, for example, Wassmer 1998). Although user fees and charges will remain an important part of local government finance, user fees and charges are unlikely to continue to increase.[6] Indeed, revenue from charges and fees will likely begin to decline, as market forces and political pressures combine to limit fees and charges. Most significantly, fees can be charged on a limited number of services. By now, most local governments have attached fees to virtually all the services that can support them. Thus, revenue can grow only as a result of increased use of services subject to fees or by increasing rates. Many observers have concluded that local governments may have maximized user fee and charges (National Conference of State Legislatures 1997a).

Utilities and Other Service-for-Fee Enterprises

Local governments also raise a significant amount of revenue from operating public utilities. The actual percentage of total revenue raised from utilities stayed fairly constant through the 1990s. In 1992, local governments raised $55 billion, or 8 percent of their total revenue, from utility income. In 1999, local governments raised approximately $77 billion, or 8 percent of their total revenue, from utilities. The most significant utilities operations engaged in by local governments in 1999 were water supply ($28 billion), electric power ($38 billion), gas supply ($4 billion), and transit services ($6 billion) (U.S. Census Bureau 2000).

Some local governments depend heavily on revenue from the operation of utilities. For example, Tallahassee, Florida, which owns an electric utility, raised 40 percent of its total revenue from selling electric power (Kelly and Ransom 2000). Tallahassee and similarly situated cities can provide relatively higher levels of public services and impose relatively lower tax burdens than localities without utility enterprises.

The primary problem with relying heavily on utility revenue is that federal and state deregulation will curtail local government operations of utilities (Walters and Cornia 1997). Federal and state deregulation of the generation and distribution of electric power severely threatens this source of revenue for local governments (Kelly and Ransom 2000).

Conclusion

Local governments have relied heavily on both intergovernmental aid and user fees and charges to finance public services, particularly since the tax revolts led to increasing limitations on taxing property. The operation of utilities by local governments has been in steady decline in an era of deregulation.

Intergovernmental aid, while politically attractive, is an economically flawed revenue source. Such aid fosters the perception that local government can be financed without local taxation. But the result of that perception can be demand for public services above and beyond what citizens are willing to pay. More important, intergovernmental aid results in a loss of political and financial control on the part of recipients. In theory, user fees and charges are among the soundest sources of revenue, and economists and public finance experts routinely encourage their use. However, because local governments have largely exploited this revenue source, few opportunities to expand user fees and charges remain.

NOTES

1. In 1957, cities relied on federal aid for 19 percent of their revenue; in 1970, cities relied on federal aid for 31 percent of their revenue (Paget 1998).

2. Local governments charge fees for hundreds of different services. A review of 30 city ordinances uncovered 135 different fees, including animal-shelter fees, tree-removal fees, museum entrance charges, and fees for police escorts at funeral processions.

3. Local governments have placed a host of different fees and charges on developers, including school impact fees, construction taxes, and community-funding fees (Dresch and Sheffrin 1997).

4. Although difficult to export, many fees are often "hidden" from those who ultimately bear the costs. For example, developers' fees are often passed on to homeowners in the form of higher housing costs.

5. Although local governments cannot charge prices beyond what the market will bear, some types of charges are set below fair market value (Bland 1997). Consistent with market theory, local governments should periodically reevaluate the prices charged for particular services.

6. Downing (1992) has argued that the role of user fees in local public finance could be greatly expanded. He argues that a doubling of user fee revenue could be expected if all local governments adopted charges at the same level of the governments charging the highest fees. Since that 1992 study, however, local governments have already doubled their use of fees and charges.

9

Financing Local Government in a Changing World

Capital is mobile, and people and business will move to places where they can keep more of it.
—Indianapolis Mayor Stephen Goldsmith, 1997

The federal system places inherent limitations on the extent and choice of taxes that American cities, towns, and counties can impose on their residents. Because individuals and firms can relocate to other areas, jurisdictions must offer competitive services and reasonable tax burdens. Local governments compete for business investment, in particular. This competition limits the taxation of mobile tax bases and the use of the tax laws to redistribute wealth.

In addition to the competitive pressure to keep taxes low, myriad political and legal limitations have constrained local taxing authority. The tax revolts of the 1970s and 1980s led to constitutional and statutory restrictions on local government taxing authority. An antitax bias has also characterized the political process at all levels of government. This bias has further restrained government financing options. Finally, many taxes that local governments rely on have inherent limitations. Sales taxes face a continually shrinking base. Personal income taxes face profound political opposition. And business taxes, many of which fall on a mobile base, have never been considered a viable source of local government revenue.

The future may very well pose even greater challenges to local government finance—and thus to local government autonomy. At the beginning of the 21st century, technological advancement, international trade, and the deregulation of utilities will magnify the traditional legal and political constraints on local tax policy. Moreover, local governments will operate in an environment shaped by constantly changing demographics.

While the world has changed rapidly, the tax systems that support all levels of governments have largely stayed the same (see, for example, Brunori 1998). The underlying taxes that support local governments were designed and implemented in a different time and for a different economy. The sales tax was first used as a temporary revenue measure during the Great Depression. Income taxes, both personal and corporate, were adopted a generation before that. The property tax has existed since the colonial period in America. With a few exceptions, these taxes have not changed significantly since their inception.[1] Most scholars believe that without radical changes, many types of taxes cannot continue raising sufficient revenue in the 21st century (Brunori 1998).

Not surprisingly, the changing economy has prompted government leaders, business leaders, and scholars to review how state and local government finance public services (see, for example, Neubig and Poddar 2000). The most significant local government review has been undertaken by the National League of Cities. In 1997, the National League of Cities launched the Municipalities in Transition Project to identify and study the economic, political, and social changes that would affect American local government. The National League of Cities has commissioned several studies on the future of local government finance (see, for example, Tannenwald 2002).

This chapter describes some of the problems and challenges posed by a rapidly changing society and economic environment as well as their likely effects on the ability of local governments to raise revenue.

Globalism

Increased international trade will continue to have profound effects on local government taxing powers. The trend of constantly increasing international trade among the nations of the world will no doubt continue (Neubig and Poddar 2000). The United States has worked diligently to encourage international trade by entering into agreements that will reduce trade barriers and encourage commerce across national borders. Local government officials are well aware of the fact that globalization will result in profound changes. As the National League of Cities (1997) reported, an

American city may conduct more trade with Hong Kong than with a direct neighbor.

Part of the increase in international trade is attributable to increases in individual and capital mobility. Falling trade barriers and dramatic reductions in communications and transportation costs have significantly increased capital mobility. The potential sites for investment and business activity have increased tremendously over the past several decades (Thomas 2000). The ability of companies and individuals to sell products and services around the world makes compliance and administration of some taxes, particularly those imposed on mobile bases, more difficult and expensive.

The problem is that most local taxes depend on physical location, even as location becomes less and less important to how people and firms do business. Income taxes are imposed according to where a person lives or works. Business taxes are imposed according to the location of sales, operations, or property. Sales and use taxes (and all consumption-based excise taxes) are determined by where the sale takes place or where the product or service is consumed. The property tax is defined by place.

International trade and ever-broadening global markets have two distinct effects on local tax policy. First, they expand competition between local governments to include foreign nations. As noted in chapter 3, state and local governments work to entice firms from neighboring states or localities to relocate. The potential to enter into bidding wars for firms exists because of the mobility of capital and lack of trade barriers within the American federal system.

The global trading network is now more open, and mobility has never been greater. Therefore, local governments are now actively involved in international economic development activities (Liou 1999). The goal of many local governments is to lure foreign companies interested in investing in the United States.

International competition extends to all levels of government. For example, counties now vigorously pursue foreign investment. More than half of all counties actively engage in enticing foreign business to their communities through trade missions and advertising campaigns aimed at foreign nationals (Pammer 1996).

International competition for business will likely center on tax policy. As in domestic competition, state and local governments will use various "selling" points to lure foreign investors. In addition to offering quality public services, particularly transportation, local governments will paint a picture of a competitive tax environment.

Local governments are aware that "in a world of mobile tax bases, inter-jurisdictional tax differentials can influence the location of such bases" (Oakland 1994, 202). Indeed, as in the case of domestic competition, the widespread perception is that lowering tax burdens, especially those related to business activities, is imperative to get foreign nationals to invest in a particular jurisdiction. Many local governments are willing to surrender tax options as part of a strategy to enhance development through increased foreign investment (Liou 1999).

State governments are competing on the international economic scene as well. State competition for foreign investment may cause additional problems for local governments. When state governments pursue companies or industries looking for investment options, the states routinely offer tax incentives. These tax incentives often consist of property tax benefits. The problem, as noted in chapter 4, is that while states are happy to compromise the local tax base, they are less excited about reimbursing local governments for their loss. In the end, the effects of competition on the way local governments raise revenue may pale in comparison to the effects of international competition.

The second issue confronting local governments in the new global marketplace is the proliferation of international trade agreements and treaties. By design, such agreements diminish or eliminate trade barriers and increase commercial activities across national borders. In doing so, however, these agreements place restrictions on the use of tax policy to finance government, particularly as tax policy relates to economic development.

Some evidence suggests that the major trade agreements signed by the United States, including the North American Free Trade Agreement (NAFTA) and the General Agreement on Tariffs and Trade (GATT), restrict state and local taxing power (Aune 2001; McLure and Hellerstein 2002). NAFTA, the World Trade Organization, GATT, and Mercosur have increased trade competition but reduced tax competition (Youngman 1999a). State and local government officials are concerned not only about a reduction in competition but also about the likelihood that state and local taxes will be challenged under international trade agreements (Carlson 1996; Hope 1994).

Finally, the idea of state and local governments competing in the international economic arena has led to calls for increased federal preemption for trade policy. Some scholars and policymakers believe that the federal government should prevent, or at least limit, state and local government involvement in international economic development (Thomas 2000). Specifically, they have called for the federal government to preempt states and local governments from pursuing foreign businesses. Although such preemption does not seem likely, it reflects the anxiety and concerns that many policymakers and political leaders have with international trade and local government finance.

The primary effect of growing international trade will be recognition that taxation of mobile capital and people is an inefficient and ineffective means of raising local government revenue. Similar to concerns over domestic competition, concerns over international competition will likely lead to the conclusion that only property taxes and user fees are capable of efficiently supporting local government.

Technological Advances

Like globalization, technological advances will continue to have profound effects on local government finance. The high-technology economy will change the way local governments raise revenue. Technology is creating new business structures, new services, and more "remote" activities (Neubig and Poddar 2000). For example, the Internet makes it possible for relatively small businesses to expand their base and to sell goods and services throughout the United States. These businesses are highly mobile and have few geographic constraints. Small and medium-sized businesses are no longer limited to local markets.

As noted in chapter 6, the ability to purchase goods and services through the Internet has sharply reduced reliance on sales taxes. Although this problem is much more serious for state than for local governments, it calls into question whether local governments can view sales taxes as an adequate source of revenue. Local governments are expected to lose tens of billions of dollars a year in sales tax revenue (Bruce and Fox 2001).

Electronic commerce will also make it much more difficult to impose business taxes. Technological developments have made businesses increasingly mobile. Businesses today are no longer as dependent on plants and equipment. Thus, relocating to another jurisdiction, while still a significant undertaking, is much easier today than it was a decade ago. This mobility will prevent expanded reliance on business taxes and will likely result in an eventual elimination of all local business taxes, as governments realize that such taxes are perceived to hurt their competitiveness. Local governments will not be able to rely on business property tax revenue to the extent they once did.

Technology will affect personal income and wage taxes as well. The age of electronic commerce has resulted in more people working from remote locations. The Internet, personal digital assistants, cell phones, and laptop computers allow employees in many industries to perform their responsibilities away from the employer's main office. Remote workers may pose challenges to local governments relying heavily on wage taxes. Employees and employers may have opportunities to avoid wage and payroll taxes. If the local government imposes taxes according to the location where the employee performs work, such opportunities will certainly exist.

To the surprise of many, the high-technology economy is also affecting local property taxes. When heavy manufacturing dominated the American economy, a large portion of the property tax base consisted of business land, plants, and equipment. Factories and heavy equipment, as well as extensive business ownership of land, have filled the coffers of local government for much of the 20th century.

Modern businesses, which tend to rely on computers and technology, have fewer plants and less equipment relative to large manufacturing firms (Bonnet 1998). These businesses do not own significant amounts of real property; this lack of ownership leads to a decrease in business property tax revenue. It also leads to a shift in property tax burdens from business to residential property (Strauss 2001).

The new economy creates another problem for the property tax. Capital-intensive firms (that is, those with relatively large amounts of plants and equipment) now incur a larger burden of the property tax than high-technology or service-centered businesses (Green, Chevrin, and Lippard 2002). That inequity ultimately undermines support for the tax, particularly within the business community. Such inequities lead to calls for lower tax burdens on capital-intensive firms.

Most commentators agree that changing technology will increase the limitations on local taxing authority (Break 2000). For this reason, researchers have cited growth in technology as one of the major factors affecting American local governments in general, and cities in particular (National League of Cities 1998).

Deregulation

Deregulation of key industries,[2] such as electricity, gas, telecommunications, and financial services, is also forcing changes in state and local business tax systems (Bonnet 1998; Burling 2000; Cline 2002; Hassell 2000; Neubig and Poddar 2000). The era of deregulation presents several issues for local government finance.

First, compared with unregulated businesses, regulated industries have traditionally been subject to higher property and other tax burdens. Local governments collect tax on gas, electric, and telecommunications utilities that are set at more than double the rate imposed on other industries (Walters and Cornia 1997). Local governments had the opportunity to impose higher tax burdens because the regulated industries were monopolies that faced little or no threat from lower-priced competitors. Utilities usually passed on the tax burdens to consumers through government-sanctioned price increases.

Today, however, deregulated industries such as power and telecommunications companies are demanding lower tax burdens more in line with the taxes paid by their new, unregulated competitors (Bonnet 1998). Moreover, falling utility prices have depressed the value of utility-owned land across the United States (Walters and Cornia 1997). This decline in value has, in turn, depressed property tax revenue across the United States. Future declines are predicted to be significant, particularly on property that is taxed to fund public education (Walters and Cornia 2001).

Second, as noted in chapter 8, many local governments own and operate utilities that provide services, usually electricity, to their residents. Most electric utilities operating in the United States are owned by cities, and the profits of the operations are used to fund general government services. Tallahassee, Florida, for example, finances 40 percent of its budget through a city-owned utility that sells electricity. The deregulation movement threatens the existence of such locally owned utilities. For those utilities that remain in operation, deregulation will change. Even if local governments maintain ownership and operation of utilities, competition from private companies is likely to decrease the revenue yield.

Finally, increased competition from the private sector will force local governments to revisit their policies concerning rights-of-way and franchise fees. Such fees and charges generate significant amounts of revenue for many localities. The inability to collect such fees will have a significant effect on nontax revenue collection (Bonnet 1998; Green et al. 2002).

Overall, the deregulation movement will likely reduce utility revenue as well as curb property tax revenue. The expected reduction in overall local government revenues will be modest, but any additional undermining of already weak traditional local tax bases could cripple local governments' ability to finance services (Walters and Cornia 1997).

An Aging Population

In addition to international trade, technology, and deregulation, the rapid aging of the U.S. population will challenge the financing capacity of local governments. Declining birth rates and longer life spans are the primary reasons for increases in the average age of Americans. In 1980, 11 percent of the U.S. population was over the age of 65. By 2030, projections show that 20 percent of the population will be older than 65 (Bonnet 1998).

Traditionally, older citizens have been thought to harbor animosity toward taxes in general, and property taxes in particular. Their animosity toward the property tax is well known (Green et al. 2002). Real estate values, and the attendant increased property tax burdens, often increase at faster rates than income, especially for elderly homeowners on fixed incomes. The property tax imposes a greater, and more visible, burden on senior citizens than any other levy.

In addition to the financial burdens imposed, property taxes are unpopular with senior citizens because of the fear that they will lose their homes if they are unable to pay property taxes. One way to enforce the property tax is to seize the property. A home, often the most valuable financial asset owned by senior citizens, has immeasurable psychological and emotional value. The thought of losing such an asset adds to homeowners' dislike of the property tax.

There has also been a widespread perception that most senior citizens are unwilling to support elementary and secondary public education. The underlying theory is that because senior citizens do not have children in the schools, they have less at stake in educational outcomes. School taxes, of course, account for the majority of property taxes. Senior citizens are thought to oppose candidates who advocate higher school taxes. Moreover, in many states, particularly in the Northeast, school budgets must be approved by a referendum of voters. Historically, the elderly have voted at far higher rates than the rest of the population. As noted in chapter 5, if the property tax is not viewed as a principal source of finance for public schools, a main rationale—and public support—for the tax evaporates. To the extent that the increasingly aging population is unwilling to support public education, that population can be expected to oppose property tax increases.

As noted in chapter 5, many of the problems that gave rise to the elderly's dislike of the property tax have been addressed by policymakers. Circuit breakers, homestead exemptions, deferrals, and other programs have significantly reduced the tax burdens on senior homeowners, particularly those with low and fixed incomes. Despite the varied relief programs, however, senior citizen animosity toward the tax continues.

Policymakers have access to few additional policies that would provide senior citizens with property tax relief. Current relief measures are already becoming increasingly expensive. Tax relief measures were instituted during a time when senior citizens had higher poverty rates than the rest of the nation. Today, however, senior citizens have the lowest poverty rates of any age group in the United States.

Tax Policy in the New Economy

The changing economy will have significant effects on local government taxation. International trade and the high-technology economy place a premium on mobility and intangible property. Local governments have never succeeded in raising money from taxing mobile capital, services, or intangibles. And no local government has devised a workable method for taxing these components of the new economy in the future.

Globalization, international trade, and technological developments will make it more difficult to rely on sales and income taxes. These developments will also make it virtually impossible for local governments to tax business activity. Business tax bases have grown far too mobile. Cities and counties are not likely to try to impose additional sales, income, and business taxes; rather, they will likely concentrate on raising revenue from immobile tax bases. One noted observer drew an analogy between the modern technological revolution and the economic transformations of the late 1800s: "It is not a paradox that the rising importance of intangible property in the 19th century led not to greater inclusion of intangibles in the tax base, but to just the opposite—restriction of the property tax base to tangible property and immobile tangible property at that" (Youngman 1999a, 1897).

In this regard, the rising importance of mobility will likely lead to increased efforts to tax immobile bases. The difficulty in taxing mobile tax bases leaves only property taxes and user fees as viable sources of revenue for local governments. These sources of revenue allow fiscal—and political—autonomy. But the tax on real property is the only tax capable of raising revenue that can sustain local government operations. As one leading theorist explains, "Real property offers one of the few tax bases that cannot be realistically shifted to another jurisdiction" (Youngman 1999a, 1898).

The changing world order, however, presents challenges to the property tax system as well. Deregulation will have a serious, albeit relatively short-term, impact on local government tax revenue. The greater challenge will come from an aging population, because older people have traditionally opposed property taxes.

In 1997, two American political scientists observed that "The hyper mobility of capital, the international division of labor, and the 'death of distance' due to information technologies appear to undermine local autonomy" (Clarke and Gaile 1997). Without the ability to increase reliance on the property tax, local autonomy will likely continue to erode.

NOTES

1. Perhaps the most significant change occurred with respect to the property tax. Until the early 20th century, the tax was levied on all property, including personal and intangible property. The "general" property tax was widely criticized as unworkable in an increasingly mobile society; this view led to widespread reforms. The property tax is now almost exclusively levied on land and improvements.

2. The most significant changes with respect to electric utilities occurred with the passage of the Federal Energy Policy Act of 1992, which requires owners of transmission lines to allow others to use their lines (Cappellari 1999). The most significant change with respect to the telecommunications industry was the enactment of the Federal Telecommunications Act of 1996 (Richman 2002).

10

A Blueprint for Strengthening the Property Tax

Local government needs a productive source of revenue they can control. . . . The property tax is well established in that role.

—George Break, 2000

At the dawn of the 21st century, American localism is at a crossroads. The system of local government has served the nation well. Local autonomy, both fiscal and political, has resulted in a federal system capable of ensuring democratic processes and providing public services in an efficient and effective manner. The history of the United States has been shaped largely by its varied and diverse system of local governments.

Today, however, the local fiscal and political autonomy that gave rise to unprecedented wealth and freedom in the United States is being challenged. This chapter reviews those challenges and describes their likely effects on how local governments raise revenue. It then provides recommendations for tax policies designed to strengthen the role localities play in governing American society, while at the same time ensuring a fair, efficient, and accountable tax system.

Challenges to Local Tax Policy and Political Autonomy

Legal, political, and economic constraints limit the means by which local governments can raise revenue. Local government's ability to rely on property tax, the most effective and efficient means of raising own-source revenue, has slowly eroded over the past several decades. The property tax system as it is now structured in most states is incapable of financing local government to the same extent it once did. The current political and legal limitations on the property tax will keep local governments from increasing their reliance on this revenue source in the near future. Without significant reforms, the property tax's role in financing public services will continue to shrink.

The alternative tax sources discussed in chapters 6 and 7 have proved inadequate substitutes for the property tax. The local-option sales tax is limited by the inability of local governments to tax services and necessities, by interjurisdictional competition, and by the various problems associated with remote sales in general and electronic commerce in particular. Although the sales tax remains the second most important source of local tax revenue, its future, like that of its state counterpart, remains in jeopardy.

The local-option income tax, while theoretically attractive as long as it is tied closely to state income taxes, suffers from intense political opposition. The perception that local income taxes deter economic growth and lead wealthy residents to relocate has created a political bias against the tax at all levels of government. The bias is particularly strong among state legislators charged with authorizing local-option income taxes. Only two states—Ohio and Pennsylvania—rely heavily on local-option income taxes.

The nontax alternatives described in chapter 8 have been the main source of replacement revenue for local governments. As noted, however, these nontax sources are inadequate substitutes for own-source tax revenue. User fees and charges, two efficient and effective means of raising revenue, are incapable of financing a large portion of government services. In addition, governments cannot impose user fees and charges on public goods that are readily available without limiting some citizens' access to them. The growth of revenue from user fees and charges also depends on two problematic strategies: increasing the use of the underlying public service or increasing rates. Increasing use is impractical because of safety and cost issues; increasing rates further limits citizen access and entails significant political and economic risks.

The intergovernmental aid system has proved unreliable. Federal aid to local governments, once thought the salvation of large cities, has practically disappeared. State aid, which now accounts for a substantial portion of all local government budgets, is a poor substitute for own-source revenue. State aid depends on the legislature, and it can be increased or decreased with little input from individual cities and counties. Citizens desiring more revenue for local services have far less influence on state policymakers. Moreover, when facing their own budget deficits, states have routinely cut aid to local governments. State aid has not proved a reliable source of revenue. And more important, state aid has the additional drawback of curbing both fiscal and political autonomy.

The challenges local governments face in practicing effective tax policy will likely increase. Demographic, technological, and economic changes are affecting all aspects of local government. As noted in chapter 9, increased international trade, deregulation, electronic commerce, and an aging population will have serious consequences for local governments. These factors will further hamper local governments' ability to raise revenue.

Without significant changes, local governments' capacity to raise and rely on their own revenue will continue to diminish. Without a viable revenue source, localities will be forced to rely on the state to fund more public services. State governments are already funding a greater share of elementary and secondary education, a trend that is likely to continue. States are also increasingly paying for local transportation services.

The greater reliance on state aid is a dangerous trend. Without an independent revenue source, local governments have limited control over policies and services in their areas, to the detriment of American federalism. Local governments can be more responsive to area needs because they have greater ability to assess and more flexibility in providing the services demanded by their citizens. Local government is more efficient at providing local services because local government officials know the costs and benefits of those services. Relying on state political leaders to pay for local police, fire protection, ambulances, and schools puts the funding of those services at risk.

More broadly, state funding can jeopardize local control. All state (and federal) aid comes with rules and regulations about how the money should be spent. Governors and lawmakers will have a greater say in how money sent to cities, towns, and counties should be used. The historical record suggests that such strings accompany all forms of financial centralization. Funding that comes with stipulations can affect such aspects of local life as the kinds of books shelved in the local library, the bias of school curricula, and the type of artwork adorning local public buildings.

Increased state funding also creates long-term uncertainties for local government finance. State political leaders will be forced to decide among competing interests. For example, when states run budget surpluses, as they did in the 1990s, politicians cut taxes. But the excess revenue may be better spent on local public services. When states run budget deficits, however, few state lawmakers are likely to increase taxes to support local public services. State financial control of local government could compromise local interests.

Recommendations for Strengthening Local Tax Autonomy

Local governments must have a dependable source of revenue that they control and that can raise sufficient revenue. Only the property tax can play that role. As one study notes, "It is imperative that property taxes become an acceptable revenue source for local governments. It is also imperative that local governments devote adequate resources to its administration. If not, local government will face a fragile revenue base, a base not capable of raising revenue in a reliable, compassionate and competent manner" (Bowman, MacManus, and Mikesell 1992, 322). Similar sentiments can be heard from most public finance experts who have studied local finance.

Under current conditions, the importance of property taxes in local government finance will continue to diminish. To reverse this trend, the tax must be strengthened and revitalized. Property tax reforms can help ensure that the local government system remains vibrant and effective. The following five steps could lead to a more viable property tax and ensure that American citizens can govern their affairs through local systems.

To some, these recommendations may seem unattainable. Indeed, they may seem utopian. They certainly will require a level of political courage and leadership rarely seen in the tax policy arena. But without significant reforms, local governments will continue to cede control over basic local services to the state.

Educate the Public on the Virtues of the Property Tax

Perhaps the most important first step in strengthening the property tax is educating the public about the many virtues of this particular revenue source. Finance experts must help change the public's perception of the property tax as "the worst tax."

Given the long history of animus toward the tax, such a suggestion may seem daunting, indeed politically impossible. But upon closer examination, changing the public's views on the property tax may not seem far-fetched.

Policymakers have addressed most of the problems that have plagued the property tax (Dearborn 1993). Virtually all states have implemented safeguards to protect individuals most vulnerable to rapidly rising property tax burdens. Low- and fixed-income homeowners now enjoy myriad protections, such as circuit breakers, homestead exemptions, and rate rollbacks. These policies have reduced property tax burdens by billions of dollars. Many states have provided additional safeguards to senior citizens. Deferral systems allow the elderly to postpone property tax payments until their death or the sale of their property.

The administration of the tax, particularly with respect to valuation procedures, has improved dramatically over the years (Mields 1993). While still imperfect, the administration is fairer and more accurate than in the past. Computer systems allow for information retrieval and mass appraisals.

In short, government reforms, many brought about by popular discontent, have largely addressed the causes of the public's real or perceived unhappiness with the property tax. Yet the tax remains unpopular with the public (Brunori 2002; Kincaid and Cole 2001).

But researchers should reconsider how they conduct public opinion polling on taxes. The public clearly does not like taxes. When asked which taxes they dislike the most, the tendency is to name those most visible—the federal income tax and the property tax. Arguably the only conclusion one can draw from such polling is that the public does not like visible taxes. But the polling generally does not link the underlying public services to the property tax. There is widespread support for basic local services such as police and education. People have routinely indicated that they are willing to pay for such services.

The unpopularity of the tax also stems from political leaders and scholars, many of whom characterize the tax as the "worst" tax. As noted in chapter 5, candidates for state office often advocate reductions in, or even abolition of, the property tax. These campaigns against the property tax persist because many politicians perceive that taxing property is inherently wrong. Campaigns against the tax fuel that perception (Youngman 2002a).

While the property tax has its share of opponents, few public finance experts defend the tax publicly. This may stem from the fact that scholars have been decidedly absent in the debate over local fiscal and political autonomy in general.

Political leaders and, more important, the public often overlook the positive aspects of the tax: it provides a steady stream of revenue to pay for local public services; it entails minimal compliance and administrative costs; it is almost impossible for property owners to evade; and it is visible—residents know what they are paying and can evaluate what they are getting in return. Most important, the public must realize that property taxes support arguably the most important services they receive, and citizens can control the quantity and quality of those services if they control the property tax. Local government cannot raise revenue any other way.[1]

Fischel (2001b) contends that people will support the property tax if they perceive that the revenue raised from the tax will support services that will ultimately increase their property values. Public opinion data show strong support for local government services, such as public safety and education, which the property tax can finance. These services should be, according to the polls, under the control of local governments.

But the public is often under the inaccurate impression that the property tax will deter first-time homeowners. In fact, since the property tax is capitalized into housing prices, higher property taxes result in decreased housing prices—a result that benefits first-time homebuyers (Youngman 2002b, 1058). In the long run, the public services paid for by those property tax increases will have the beneficial effect of increasing property values.

Organizations such as the Lincoln Institute of Land Policy have largely spurred educational efforts to better inform the political leadership and the public about the benefits of the property tax (Brunori 2001d). But it is time for other organizations with a connection to policymakers to join the effort. For example, the National League of Cities, the National Conference of State Legislatures, and the National Association of Counties could help educate more people about the use of the property tax. Organizations representing school districts, school boards, and teachers unions—whose public services are best funded by the property tax— could also have an impact. Moreover, a broader effort to help the public understand government finance and the need to maintain stable revenue sources could encompass initiatives to boost the public's understanding of the property tax. If the public better understood the link between property taxes and fundamental public services, such as local public safety and schools, opposition toward the tax would diminish.

Ease the Excesses of the Property Tax Revolts

Educating the public and political leaders is only the first step toward strengthening the property tax. The property tax will be unable to provide a stable, dependable source of revenue for local governments as long as the most draconian limitations from the tax revolt era remain in place. If the property tax is to be strengthened, the excesses of the property tax revolts must be reversed. What is needed is essentially a property tax "counterrevolt" (Brunori 2001d).[2]

The tax revolts, while politically popular, have not resulted in sound tax policy. For example, property tax rate and assessment limitations have little economic or tax policy justification. Such limits keep property tax revenue artificially low, increase administrative costs, and shift the burden of paying for government to other types of taxes, other levels of government, and other taxpayers. Rate limits curb local political control even in jurisdictions that allow voters to override the limits. Assessment limitations foster horizontal inequities; neighbors with similar home values may bear radically different tax burdens. Possible policy solutions can include raising or eliminating reassessment limits, particularly for business property, and raising or eliminating rate limitations (see Sexton, Sheffrin, and O'Sullivan 1999).

Under a sound tax system, taxes serve one goal: to raise adequate revenue to pay for the government services citizens demand. The current restrictions on property taxes prevent the tax from being used to fund the services demanded by the citizens.

Citizens and organizations that value public services must take the lead. The first step is to convince the public of the problems created by the tax revolts. Citizens often believed that tax limitations would have little or no effect on public services (Citrin 1979; O'Sullivan 2000). According to some researchers, however, tax limitations have reduced the level and effectiveness of public services, particularly education (Downes and Figlio 1999; Downes, Dye, and McGuire 1998; Figlio 1997).

The public's goal in supporting the tax revolts was to reduce tax burdens—not to reduce government services (Courant, Gramlich, and Rubinfeld 1980). Moreover, some evidence suggests that citizens regret the imposition of tax limits (Cutler, Elmendorf, and Zeckhauser 1999;

O'Sullivan 2000). More important, the tax revolts led to the increased state centralization of local public finance. This centralization has, in turn, led directly to an increase in state tax burdens as well as a decrease in local autonomy.

Most important, some evidence suggests that the bulk of the tax relief created by the tax revolts went to those who needed it the least. Wealthy homeowners and corporate business interests were the beneficiaries of the tax limitations (see, for example, Goldberg 2000; Kuttner 1980).

A call to reverse tax limitations may appear politically infeasible, since the public strongly supported the limitations imposed by many of the tax revolts, including the most severe limitations set in place by Proposition 13.[3] Not many politicians will call for a reversal of the laws put into place by the property tax revolts. Admittedly, it will take political leadership, as well as a commitment on the part of the public, to initiate meaningful reforms.

Not all of the policies implemented as a result of the property tax revolts should be repealed. For example, provisions designed to protect low- and fixed-income property owners—including homestead exemptions and low-income property tax credits—should be retained. The public also needs to be better educated about these programs. Baer (1998), for example, found that property tax relief measures have not been effective because they are underused, with just 25 percent of eligible homeowners aware of the availability of tax relief programs. Another 14 percent, while aware of the tax relief programs, incorrectly believed that they were ineligible. And Youngman (2002a) has shown that local governments underuse property tax deferral programs, arguably one of the most effective means of providing relief to senior citizens without sacrificing local autonomy. Such public misperception does not improve the image of the property tax, and it renders relief efforts ineffectual.

Concerns over government revenue windfalls, especially in times of high inflation, can be addressed by retaining or adopting rate rollbacks and other measures designed to ensure that the government collects only enough revenue to meet its budgetary obligations. Support for a strong, viable property tax is not inconsistent with the idea that excess revenue should be returned to taxpayers.

Lifting rate and assessment limitations will result in greater property tax burdens—but not in every instance. The public should demand that political leaders reduce rates during times of rapidly rising property values. Had California local governments reduced rates in the 1970s, when property tax revenue was increasing far faster than the costs of government, they might have forestalled or even prevented the passage of Proposition 13.

To make property tax reforms politically palatable, increased property tax burdens should be tied to corresponding cuts in local-option sales taxes and, where possible, to cuts in local-option income taxes. Property tax reforms tied to significant decreases in state tax burdens would be even more effective. This proposition runs counter to the recent trend of increasing state tax burdens to pay for local government services. Tax revenue, whether from state or local sources, must be raised to pay for public services. Given its support of local government, the public might prefer the control that local taxes, particularly property taxes, offer.

Expand the Property Tax Base

For the property tax to provide a stable source of revenue that will ensure local autonomy, state and local governments must address the problem posed by a continuously shrinking tax base. Specifically, state and local governments must address the significant problem of exempt properties. As noted in chapter 5, exemptions for economic development and charitable organizations cost local governments billions of dollars and shift the burden of paying for public services to other taxpayers. Both types of exemptions, however, are politically popular among a public that values economic development as much as it cherishes the nation's tradition of nonprofit organizations.

Scholars, policymakers, and political leaders are capable of discussing the issues presented by these exemptions. And there is growing support for reforms that will curtail the continued loss of property tax revenue. Local governments will continue to compete; the federal system ensures that outcome. The question is how they will compete. In general, competition serves the American public by enhancing the efficiency of local government. Not all competition, however, results in efficiency gains or optimal outcomes. Some forms of competition, such as tax incentives aimed at individual firms, are harmful to the localities that engage in them.

The continuum of good and bad competition is particularly evident with respect to local tax policy. All levels of government use their tax laws as a means of fostering economic development (i.e., they compete with other jurisdictions). Ideally, such competition should take the form of overall lower tax burdens (Duncan 1992). Competition should not involve targeted tax incentives available to one or a few recipients. Despite their proliferation, targeted tax incentives are increasingly viewed as an inefficient means of creating jobs or spurring growth (Brunori 1997). Increased media coverage and the adoption of disclosure laws will shed light on some of the problems associated with targeted tax incentives. Curbing the use of targeted tax incentives would protect the property tax base, and consequently, strengthen the property tax.

The issue of exemptions for nonprofit organizations is more controversial. Religious, educational, and charitable organizations hold a special place in American society. Repealing property-tax exemptions benefiting such organizations would be extremely difficult, but state and local governments can minimize the financial impact of such exemptions.

Pomp (2002) offered several sensible policy alternatives that could better protect local government revenue within the existing legal structure. These policies include requiring local government permission before taxable property can be purchased by a tax-exempt organization; limiting the number of acres qualifying for exemption; setting dollar limits on the amount of property that can be exempt; imposing user charges on tax-exempt organizations; and having the state reimburse local governments for the costs of exemptions (Pomp 2002, 389). These efforts alone would provide significant relief to local governments throughout the United States.[4]

Address the Problems of School Finance Equalization

Strengthening the property tax means that state governments must also address the problem of fiscal inequities in education finance. As Break (2000) observes, "Reduced reliance on the local school financing is likely to continue to erode the importance of the local property tax in the our fiscal system."

The overall goal is not controversial—all children should be afforded equal educational opportunities. Unfortunately, one remedy to this significant social problem—that is, giving states greater control over education—has weakened political control at the local level, where the individual citizen has much more influence. State political leaders increasingly set the educational agenda—regardless of local preferences (Brown 1996). Many studies have shown that state-funded education is less likely to be efficient or to reflect local values (see Strauss 1995).

More important, state centralization of school finance may not work, at least not in the manner envisioned by reformers. Centralization of school finance has depressed overall funding for schools (Downes and Shah 1995; Silva and Sonstelie 1995; Theobald and Picus 1991). For example, Downes and Figlio (1999) surveyed research on the effects of tax limits and increased state centralization on education and found reductions in overall student performance. Moreover, some evidence suggests that centralization erodes support for public education (Fischel 1998; Hoxby 1998) and that centralization has not solved the problem of financial inequality among school districts (Murray, Evans, and Schwab 1998).

The effect of education finance reforms in California suggests that centralization has resulted in a significant decrease in education spending in that state (Evans, Murray, and Schwab 2001). California's per pupil education spending fell from fifth in the nation in 1965 to fortieth in 1994. Its overall spending on education over that time fell 20 percent compared with the rest of the nation's. By 1991, the state was 47th in the country in per pupil textbook spending (Youngman 1997b).

Equalization may have reduced the effectiveness of the education system, surely a result not desired by reformers. Husted and Kenny (1997) found a correlation between state funding for education and lower Scholastic Aptitude Test scores. Downes (1992) found that centralization did not improve teaching in poor districts. Downes (1997) found that increased state funding led to higher dropout rates. The evidence also suggests that equalization leads to less efficiency and effectiveness (see Hoxby 1995).

The case for fiscal equalization may be far less persuasive than originally thought by reformers. As a means of addressing inequities, it is a poorly targeted one. Oakland (1994, 207) notes, "while the objectives sought by those advocating equalization policies are noble ones, they can usually be accomplished more effectively by policies which more carefully target the problem at hand." In addition to being poorly targeted, state equalization programs are inefficient. In poor communities, after equalizing school financing, public services might appear less expensive than they really are, while in wealthier communities they might appear more expensive (Oakland 1994).

The answer is not to cede control, financial or political, to the state. Rather, political leaders should develop methods of equalizing school spending that do not include reducing local taxing authority. Elected school boards must have adequate taxing authority to lead the nation's school systems effectively and efficiently. Without such taxing authority, elected school boards are ineffectual. Many citizens recognize the connection between local taxing authority and political control of the schools (Campbell and Fischel 1996). Fischel (1998), for example, found that state legislators favor centralization more than voters do.

Evans, Murray, and Schwab (2001), for example, set forth a school-funding plan that would minimize state hegemony over local affairs. They proposed that the state guarantee all children an adequate education and provide funding to cover the costs of that education. But all local governments would be free to spend as much as they would like on education above that amount. Such an approach would enable local school districts to function more efficiently (families would be able to sort themselves according to their preferred levels of education spending). Citizens would have incentive to monitor school spending, since such spending—and the taxes levied in support thereof—would be capitalized into house values. Most important, such an approach would allow local citizens to control their school systems.

Finally, proponents of localism, and arguably sound education systems, must convince the public, particularly senior citizens, that the costs of public education are capitalized into their housing values. That is, the better the schools are, the higher the property values in the school district should be. The result is more support for education. And that makes the property tax the logical source of education financing (Strauss 2001).

Adopt a Split-Rate Property Tax System

Reforms to the property tax will be difficult to accomplish. Changing public attitudes, reversing popular tax limitation laws, and curtailing exemptions present daunting challenges. Attaining even some reforms will take much energy and commitment.

A more effective and efficient approach to strengthening the property tax system—and consequently local political autonomy—is for policy-makers and political leaders to explore an alternative way of taxing property. Today, the property tax is levied primarily on the value of the land and improvements (buildings and structures). Although this system has served the nation well, a more effective and efficient way of taxing property would be for state governments to allow localities the option of taxing land at a higher rate than improvements. Such a "split-rate" tax system would enhance local government revenue-raising capabilities. More important, as described below, adopting a land-based tax system would enable local governments to raise revenue efficiently and effectively in the new economy. And such capabilities can only strengthen local government.

Over the past several years, there has been a growing interest in the idea of split-rate taxation (Brunori 1997). Split-rate taxation is similar to the concept of land value taxation first championed by 19th-century reformer Henry George.[5] Land value taxation simply involves taxing the value of land while exempting all improvements. George recognized the efficiencies and fairness of taxing land; owners of land continue to accrue benefits after buying the land that are not based on work or further investment. Rather, the work and investment of others and the prosperity of society drive up land values. Thus, George believed that the returns property owners realize from holding land are essentially windfalls that require no economic contribution by the owner. Land value taxation does not burden investment decisions. Rather, it encourages efficient land use. Making the cost of holding land more expensive will create pressure to use the land more productively.

George envisioned exempting improvements, but taxing land to such an extent that the single land tax would replace all other taxes. Few people discuss land taxation in such terms in the 21st century. Rather, modern thinking on land taxation has centered on the concept of split-rate taxation. In a split-rate system, improvements are still subject to tax, but at lower rates than the land itself. The higher land tax rates are compared with land-improvement tax rates, which is closer to George's ideal of land taxation.

In a split-rate system, owners have an incentive to use their land as efficiently as possible. Because they are going to be taxed at a higher rate, a split-rate system gives landowners an incentive to improve the land. Moreover, because improvements are taxed at a lower rate, owners have greater incentive to build and develop the land. In other words, under a split-rate system, landowners incur lower tax costs if they develop the land than if they leave it untouched.

Financing local government using a split-rate system has many advantages in the modern economy. First, a split-rate tax system could assist local governments in meeting their dual imperatives of raising revenue to pay for basic services while fostering economic development. Many economists believe that a split-rate tax system could provide a stable, reliable source of revenue without adversely affecting economic growth.

Increasing the relative tax on land, of course, will not encourage development. Significantly, however, some evidence suggests that such an increase will not seriously hinder development (Harris 1974). Land taxation offers an exception to the rule that taxes distort economic decisions.

Reducing the tax burden on improvements, however, would significantly affect development. For local governments, especially central cities, land value taxation may be a particularly attractive source of revenue. Lower improvement taxes would create an incentive to develop underused spaces, such as empty buildings and vacant lots. It also would benefit those localities "caught in the vicious cycle of poverty with an attractive tax instrument that generates additional local government revenue without additional exodus" (Wassmer 1998).

As noted throughout this book, local governments are restricted from taxing mobile capital, firms, property, and people. Mobile tax bases can relocate to avoid tax burdens. Land, however, is immobile, and the owners cannot relocate to avoid taxes. Taxing land essentially diminishes the public finance problems associated with mobility (Wassmer 1998).

Another advantage of a split-rate tax system is the alleviation of harmful intergovernmental tax competition. The present property tax system, with its emphasis on taxing improvements, is a natural target of proponents of tax incentives. Business investment in plants and equipment leads to higher tax burdens as a result of increased property values. Thus, local governments offer, and businesses seek, property tax incentives more than any other tax inducement (Youngman 1998c). But a split-rate tax system would provide little opportunity to use tax incentives. A tax incentive will not and cannot increase the amount of land, any more than raising tax rates will decrease the amount of land.

Unlike traditional property taxes, a split-rate system already provides a natural tax incentive to build and develop. A split-rate tax system would not, at least compared to other taxes, provide a disincentive to invest in plants or equipment (Youngman 1998c). Nor would it discourage business activity.[6] For example, England (2002) found that shifting to a split-rate tax system would have a positive economic impact both in the short and long term (see also DiMasi 1987; Follain and Fernandez 1986).

Split-rate taxation has other advantages as well. This system can lead to less sprawl, as property owners develop underused land in urban areas rather than developing in rural or exurban areas. In that regard, split-rate taxation might even reduce transportation costs within a metropolitan area (Harris 1974).

Localities in the United States have implemented split-rate taxation sparingly. Several cities in Pennsylvania (Pittsburgh being the largest) adopted split-rate systems for a short time, with largely positive results. In 1980, Pittsburgh adopted a split-rate system that taxed land at a higher rate than improvements. The higher tax on land had a little or no effect on economic development in Pittsburgh. But the lower tax burdens on land improvements had a positive effect on development (Oates and Schwab 1997). Overall, the split-rate system has been credited with spurring economic development and growth in Pittsburgh.[7]

Despite its apparent success, the Pittsburgh experiment with split-rate taxation ended in 2001. The city moved to a single-rate tax system as a result of a controversial court-ordered reassessment (Catts 2002a). The reassessment resulted in a 54 percent increase in property values. The proportion of the value assigned to land increased from less than 20 percent to more than 25 percent. Land values nearly doubled. But public finance experts have faulted the reassessment as inaccurate (Catts 2002a). At the same time, political leaders took advantage of the public's unhappiness to blame the controversy on the split-rate system.

Split-rate tax systems have been adopted in many countries outside the United States. As of 2002, local governments in South Africa, Australia, New Zealand, and Canada had adopted split-rate tax systems. In some of these countries, researchers have credited split-rate taxation with fostering economic development (Schwab and Harris 1998). The concept of land taxation has even been discussed in conjunction with local finance in the People's Republic of China (Gu and Trefzger 2000).

Based on these successes, more American local governments have taken an interest in land value taxation. In 2002, the Philadelphia City Council authorized a study of split-rate taxation for possible adoption. In Virginia, the legislature in 2002 authorized Fairfax City to adopt a split-rate tax system. State and local political leaders in Virginia lauded the decision as a means of fostering more efficient land use (Catts 2002b). The Virginia legislation was aided by a feasibility study that found in a revenue-neutral split-rate system, 80 percent of homeowners would receive a tax deduction.

In 1999, the New Jersey Assembly held public hearings as part of an effort to replace the single tax rate system with a graded tax system that would tax land at higher rates than improvements (CR 145). Academics, local government officials, and business leaders all testified in favor of a split-rate tax system.

In California, interest in the concept of split-rate taxation is also growing. Goldberg (2000) notes that the current property tax system in California "stands good land use economics on its head." The 2 percent assessment limitation on all property actually reduces the cost of holding land and eliminates the incentive to build and improve vacant land.

Wholesale changes to a split-rate tax system would pose significant administrative complexities and costs, particularly for local governments with sophisticated property tax systems (Schwab and Harris 1998). An abrupt shift to split-rate taxation would be impossible (see, for example, Aaron 1975). Moreover, legislators would have to carefully implement land tax reforms designed to take into account the expectations of property owners. Politicians would also have to make the public understand why the adoption of a split-rate tax system will increase the tax burdens on some owners (Harris 1974). As one noted commentator asserted, "It may be worthwhile if they make the property tax a better proxy for the local government benefits enjoyed by owners or occupants" (Break 2000).

The concept of land taxation or its split-rate variant has wide appeal among public finance scholars. Many economists who have studied the issue have written favorably about land taxation. In 1991, a group of American economists wrote President Mikhail Gorbachev urging the Russian leader to consider land taxation as part of the reforms toward democracy and a market economy. The letter was signed by Nobel Prize winners Franco Modigliani, James Tobin, and Robert Solow, as well as William Vickrey (who was awarded the prize in 1996) and such other giants in the public finance field as Lowell Harris, Richard Musgrave, and Oliver Oldman. Many noted economists actively endorse this method of government finance (Harris 1974; Ladd 1998; Netzer 1993; Vickrey 1970).[8] From an academic perspective, the efficiency and fairness of a land-based tax system seems irrefutable.

Despite this widespread support, policymakers have not embraced the concept of land taxation. But as local governments struggle to finance public services in an increasingly mobile economy, policy leaders may want to reconsider. Split-rate tax reforms could lead to a system that raises enough revenue to pay for public services, minimizes economic disincentives, and allows local governments to maintain a satisfactory level of political control over their affairs.

In the words of one scholar, a split-rate tax may be the "magic bullet" localities need to pay for government services in the modern economy (Wassmer 1998).

NOTES

1. The percentage of local revenue raised through non-property taxes (excluding user fees) has remained constant for 40 years (Holcombe and Sobel 1997).

2. But see McGuire (1999), who argues that the effects of the tax limitation movement may be positive if it has restrained government growth that was outside the effective control of the political process.

3. In fact, public opinion polls regularly show that Californians favor the limitations imposed by Proposition 13 and, by wide margins, would vote for the constitutional amendment again.

4. There is evidence that property tax relief for owners of farmland has had little effect on preserving the family farm or preserving open space. The failure of the relief efforts should be reason to reexamine the programs. More important, if such programs continue, they should be financed exclusively by the state or federal governments. The true benefits of preserving family farms and open space go beyond the locality in which the farm is located. And the costs of such measures should likewise be shared.

5. While Henry George is most closely associated with land taxation, many leading economists, including Adam Smith, David Ricardo, and John Stuart Mill, wrote favorably about the concept.

6. A split-rate system will not be ideal for all local governments. Oates (1999b) noted, for example, that the case for land taxation in the suburbs is less compelling than it is for larger cities. But fiscal and political autonomy should allow local governments to evaluate whether split-rate taxation would work.

7. Cord (1983) found that other Pennsylvania cities have benefited from split-rate tax systems as well.

8. Even economists who do not believe it practical to adopt a pure land value tax system recognize the theoretical justification for such a system (Sheffrin 1999).

References

Aaron, Henry A. 1975. *Who Pays the Property Tax?* Washington, D.C.: Brookings Institution.

Adler, Moshe, Oliver Cook, and James Parrott. 2002. "Do Tax Increases in New York City Cause a Loss of Jobs?" *State Tax Notes* (February 4): 385–89.

Anderson, John E. 1994. *Fiscal Equalization for State and Local Government Finance.* Westport, Conn.: Praeger.

Anderson, John E., and Robert W. Wassmer. 2000. *Bidding for Business.* Kalamazoo, Mich.: W. E. Upjohn.

Aune, Katie. 2001. "Enforcing the Standards of GATT/WTO in Challenges to State Taxes." *State Tax Notes* (December 24): 1015–20.

Baer, David. 1998. "Awareness and Popularity of Property Tax Relief Programs." *Assessment Journal* 5(July/August): 47–51.

Bahl, Roy. 2001. *Fiscal Decentralization, Revenue Assignment, and the Case for the Property Tax in South Africa.* Atlanta: Georgia State University.

Bahl, Roy W., and Johannes Linn. 1992. *Urban Public Finance in Developing Countries.* New York: Oxford University Press.

Bahl, Roy, David Sjoquist, and W. Loren Williams. 1991. "School Finance Reform and Impact on Property Taxes." In *Proceedings of the Eighty-Third Annual Conference on Taxation,* edited by Frederick Stock (163–71). Columbus, Ohio: National Tax Association.

Banfield, Edward. 1961. *Political Influence.* New York: Free Press.

Bartik, Timothy J. 1991. *Who Benefits from State and Local Economic Development Policies?* Kalamazoo, Mich.: W. E. Upjohn Institute for Employment Research.

Batt, William H. 1993. "User Fees: The Nontax Revenue Alternative." *State Tax Notes* (April 5): 787–94.

Beamer, Glenn. 2000. *Creative Politics: Taxes and Public Goods in a Federal System.* Ann Arbor: University of Michigan Press.

Berman, David R. 2000. *State and Local Politics*. Armonk, N.Y.: M. E. Sharpe.

Bierhanzl, Edward J., and Paul B. Downing. 1998. "User Charges and Bureaucratic Inefficiency." *Atlantic Economic Journal* 26(June): 175–89.

Bingham, Richard D., Brett W. Hawkins, and F. Ted Hebert. 1978. *The Politics of Raising State and Local Revenue*. New York: Praeger.

Bird, Richard M. 1993. "Threading the Fiscal Labyrinth: Some Issues in Fiscal Decentralization." *National Tax Journal* 46(2): 207–27.

Bird, Richard M., and Christine Wallich. 1993. *Fiscal Decentralization and Intergovernmental Relations in Transition Economies*. Washington, D.C.: World Bank.

Bish, Robert L., and Vincent Ostrom. 1973. *Understanding Urban Government*. Washington, D.C.: American Enterprise Institute.

Bland, Robert L. 1997. "Franchise Fees and Telecommunications Services: Is a New Paradigm Needed?" *State Tax Notes* (February 10): 437–43.

Blough, Roy. 1955. *The History and Philosophy of Taxation*. Williamsburg, Va.: College of William and Mary.

Bonnet, Thomas W. 1998. *Is the New Global Economy Leaving State and Local Tax Structures Behind?* Washington, D.C.: National League of Cities.

Bowman, Ann O. 2002. "American Federalism on the Horizon." *Publius* 32(2): 3–22.

Bowman, John H., and John L. Mikesell. 1978a. "Fiscal Disparities and Local Non-Property Taxes." *Proceedings of the 70th Annual Conference on Taxation*. Washington, D.C.: National Tax Association.

———. 1978b. "Uniform Assessment of Property: Returns from Institutional Remedies." *National Tax Journal* 13(1): 137–53.

Bowman, John H., Susan MacManus, and John L. Mikesell. 1992. "Mobilizing Resources for Public Services: Financing Urban Government." *Journal of Urban Affairs* 14(3/4): 311–35.

Boyd, Donald J. 2000. "State Fiscal Issues and Risks at the Start of a New Century." *State Tax Notes* (September 11): 691–713.

Break, George. 1980. *Financing Government in a Federal System*. Washington, D.C.: Brookings Institution.

———. 1993. "State-Local Tax Policy: A Supportive, Complementary Framework." *State Tax Notes* (March 29): 720.

———. 1995. "The Local Property Tax: Falling Star or Rising Phoenix?" *State Tax Notes* (October 9): 1060–61.

———. 2000. "The New Economy and the Old Tax System." *State Tax Notes* (March 6): 767–71.

Briffault, Richard. 1990a. "Our Localism, Part I: The Structure of Local Government Law." *Columbia Law Review* 90(1): 2.

———. 1990b. "Our Localism, Part II: Localism and Legal Theory." *Columbia Law Review* 90(2): 346.

———. 1997. "The Law and Economics of Federalism." *Minnesota Law Review* 82(2): 503.

Brody, Evelyn. 2002. *Property-Tax Exemption for Charities*. Washington, D.C.: Urban Institute Press.

Brown, Dorothy. 1996. "Deconstructing Local Control: Ohio's Contribution." *Capital University Law Review* 25(1).

Brown, Tom. 2000. "Constitutional Tax and Expenditure Limitation in Colorado: The Impact on Municipal Governments." *Public Budgeting and Finance* 20(3): 29–50.

Bruce, Donald, and William F. Fox. 2001a. "E-Commerce and Local Finance: Estimates of Direct and Indirect Sales Tax Losses." *Municipal Finance Journal* 22(fall): 24–47.

———. 2001b. "State and Local Sales Tax Revenue Losses from E-Commerce: Updated Estimates." *State Tax Notes* (October 15): 203–14.

Brueckner, Jan K. 1983. "Property Value Maximization and Public Sector Efficiency." *Journal of Urban Economics* 14(July): 1–15.

Brunori, David. 1997. "Principles of Tax Policy and Targeted Tax Incentives." *State and Local Government Review* 29(1): 50–61.

———. 1998. *The Future of State Taxation.* Washington, D.C.: Urban Institute Press.

———. 1999. "Did Tax Base Sharing Fall Prey to the Suburban Sharks?" *State Tax Notes* (February 8): 401–2.

———. 2001a. "The Politics of State Taxation: Battling over Local Option Taxes." *State Tax Notes* (April 16): 1363–66.

———. 2001b. "The Politics of State Taxation: Political, Legal Crises Plague School Finance." *State Tax Notes* (January 29): 339–40.

———. 2001c. "The Politics of State Taxation: This Property Tax Problem Is Likely to Get Worse." *State Tax Notes* (December 3): 751–52.

———. 2001d. "To Preserve Local Government, It's Time to Save the Property Tax." *State Tax Notes* (September 10): 813–18.

———. 2001e. *State Tax Policy: A Political Perspective.* Washington, D.C.: Urban Institute Press.

———. 2002. "The Politics of State Taxation: Talking 'bout Real Taxes." *State Tax Notes* (August 5): 425–27.

Bryce, James. 1921. *Modern Democracies.* London: Macmillan.

Buchanan, James M. 1971. "Principles of Urban Fiscal Strategy." *Public Choice* 11(1): 1–16.

Burling, Phillip. 2000. *Impacts of Electric Utility Deregulation on the Property Tax.* Cambridge, Mass.: Lincoln Institute of Land Policy.

Campbell, Colin D., and William Fischel. 1996. "Preference for School Finance Systems: Voters versus Judges." *National Tax Journal* 49(1): 1–15.

Cappellari, John. 1999. "Electric Utility Taxation under Deregulation." *State Tax Notes* (January 18): 177–94.

Carlson, Keith. 1996. "Implications of GATT and NAFTA for Minnesota's Sales and Use Tax." *State Tax Notes* (February 19): 599–603.

Cashin, Sheryll D. 2000. "Localism, Self-Interest, and the Tyranny of the Favored Quarter: Addressing the Barriers to New Regionalism." *Georgetown Law Journal* 88(1985).

Catts, Timothy. 2002a. "Pittsburgh, Philadelphia Mull Past, Future Property Tax Reforms." *State Tax Today* (January 23): 16.22.

———. 2002b. "Virginia House Approves Split Rate Property Tax for Fairfax City." *State Tax Today* (January 30): 22.58.

Citrin, Jack. 1979. "Do People Want Something for Nothing? Public Opinion on Taxes and Spending." *National Tax Journal* 32(2): 113–30.

Clarke, Susan, and Gary Gaile. 1997. "Local Politics in a Global Era: Thinking Locally, Acting Globally." *Annals of the Academy of Political and Social Science* 551(May): 28–43.

Cline, Robert. 2002. "Can the Current State and Local Business Tax System Survive the New Economy Challenges?" *State Tax Notes* (April 15): 241–46.

Coleman, Henry A., James W. Hughes, and David Kehler. 2001. *Fiscal Responsibility.* New Brunswick: The Fund for New Jersey.

Conlan, Timothy. 1998. *From New Federalism to Devolution.* Washington, D.C.: Brookings Institution.

Cord, Steven B. 1983. "Taxing Land More than Buildings: The Record in Pennsylvania." In *The Property Tax and Local Finance,* edited by C. Lowell Harris (172–79). New York: The Academy of Political Science.

Cordes, Joseph, Marie Gantz, and Thomas Pollak. 2002. "What Is the Property-Tax Exemption Worth?" In *Property-Tax Exemption for Charities,* edited by Evelyn Brody (81–112). Washington, D.C.: Urban Institute Press.

Cornia, Gary C., and Gloria Wheeler. 1999. "The Personal Property Tax." In *Handbook on Taxation,* edited by W. Bartley Hildreth and James A. Richardson (119–48). New York: Marcel Dekker, Inc.

Cornia, Gary C., Kelly D. Edmiston, Steven M. Sheffrin, Terri A. Sexton, David L. Sjoquist, and C. Kurt Zorn. 2000. "An Analysis of the Feasibility of Implementing a Single Rate Sales Tax." *National Tax Journal* 53(4): 1327–50.

Courant, Paul, Edward Gramlich, and Daniel Rubinfeld. 1980. "Why Voters Support Tax Limitations: The Michigan Case." *National Tax Journal* 33(1): 1–20.

Crapo, John R. 2001. *The Impact of the Payroll Tax in San Francisco. A Report to the San Francisco Chamber of Commerce.* San Francisco: San Francisco Chamber of Commerce.

Croteau, Roger. 2002. "New Tax Law Worries Comal." *San Antonio Express-News,* 15 May, 1.

Cutler, David M., Douglas W. Elmendorf, and Richard Zeckhauser. 1999. "Restraining the Leviathan: Property Tax Limitation in Massachusetts." *Journal of Public Economics* 71(3): 313–34.

Dahl, Robert. 1961. *Who Governs? Democracy and Power in an American City.* New Haven, Conn.: Yale University Press.

Dearborn, Philip M. 1993. "Local Property Taxes, Emerging Trends." *Intergovernmental Perspective* (summer): 10–12.

DeLeon, Richard. 1992. *Left Coast City: Progressive Politics in San Francisco, 1975–1991.* Lawrence: University Press of Kansas.

DiMasi, Joseph A. 1987. "The Effects of Site Value Taxation in and Urban Area." *National Tax Journal* 40(4): 577–90.

Downes, Thomas A. 1992. "Evaluating the Impact of School Finance Reform on the Provision of Public Education: The California Case." *National Tax Journal* 45(4): 405–19.

———. 1997. "The Effect of *Serrano v. Priest* on the Quality of American Education." *1996 Proceedings of the Eighty-Ninth Annual Conference on Taxation.* Washington, D.C.: National Tax Association.

Downes, Thomas A., and David N. Figlio. 1999. "Do Tax and Expenditure Limits Provide a Free Ride? Evidence on the Link between Limits and Public Sector Quality." *National Tax Journal* 52(1): 113–28.

Downes, Thomas, and Mona Shah. 1995. "The Effects of School Finance Reforms on the Level and Growth of Per Pupil Expenditures." Discussion Paper 95-05, Department of Economics. Medford, Mass.: Tufts University.

Downes, Thomas A., Richard F. Dye, and Therese Mcguire. 1998. "Do Limitations Matter? Evidence on the Effects of Tax Limitations on School Performance." *Journal of Urban Economics* 43(3): 401–17.

Downing, Paul B. 1992. "The Revenue Potential of User Charges in Municipal Finance." *Public Finance Quarterly* 20(4): 512–25.

———. 1999. "User Charges, Impact Fees, and Service Charges." In *Handbook on Taxation*, edited by W. Bartley Hildreth and James A. Richardson (239–62). New York: Marcel Dekker, Inc.

Dresch, Marla, and Steven M. Sheffrin. 1997. "The Role of Development Fees and Exactions in Local Public Finance." *State Tax Notes* (December 1): 1411–16.

Duncan, Harley. 1992. "Interstate Tax Competition: The Good, the Bad, and the Ugly." *State Tax Notes* (August 24): 266–70.

Dye, Richard, and Therese McGuire. 1997. "The Effect of Property Tax Limitation Measures on Local Government Fiscal Behavior." *Journal of Public Economics* 66(3): 469–87.

Elkin, Stephen L. 1987. *City and Regime in the American Republic*. Chicago: University of Chicago Press.

England, Richard W. 2002. "Land Value Taxation and Local Economic Development: Results of a Simulation Study." *State Tax Notes* (April 22): 323–27.

Evans, William, Sheila Murray, and Robert M. Schwab. 2001. "The Property Tax and Education Finance." In *Property Taxation and Local Government Finance*, edited by Wallace E. Oates (209–35). Cambridge, Mass.: Lincoln Institute of Land Policy.

Figlio, David N. 1997. "Did the 'Tax Revolt' Reduce School Performance?" *Journal of Public Economics* 65(3): 245–69.

Figlio, David N., and Arthur O'Sullivan. 2001. "The Local Response to Tax Limitation Measures: Do Local Governments Manipulate Voters to Increase Revenues?" *Journal of Law and Economics* 44(1): 233–58.

Fischel, William. 1979. "Determinants of Voting on Environmental Quality." *Journal of Environmental Economics and Management* 6(June): 107–18.

———. 1989. "Did Serrano Cause Proposition 13?" *National Tax Journal* 42(4): 465–73.

———. 1995. *Regulatory Takings: Law, Economics and Politics*. Cambridge: Harvard University Press.

———. 1998. "School Finance Litigation and Property Tax Revolts: How Undermining Local Control Turns Voters Away from Public Education." Working Paper. Cambridge, Mass.: Lincoln Institute of Land Policy.

———. 2001a. *The Homevoter Hypothesis: How Home Values Influence Local Government Taxation, School Finance, and Land-Use Policies*. Cambridge: Harvard University Press.

———. 2001b. "Municipal Corporations, Homeowners, and the Benefit View of the Property Tax." In *Property Taxation and Local Government Finance*, edited by Wallace E. Oates (33–78). Cambridge, Mass.: Lincoln Institute of Land Policy.

Fisher, Glenn W. 1989. "Property Taxes and Local Government: Four Hypotheses." *Journal of Property Taxation* 8(2): 113–28.

———. 1996. *The Worst Tax?* Lawrence: University of Kansas Press.

Follain, James R., and Tamar Fernandez. 1986. "Land Versus Capital Value Taxation." *National Tax Journal* 39(3): 451–70.

Fox, William. 1998. "Can the State Sales Tax Survive a Future Like Its Past?" In *The Future of State Taxation*, edited by David Brunori (33–48). Washington, D.C.: Urban Institute Press.

Frug, Gerald E. 1980. "The City as a Legal Concept." *Harvard Law Review* 93(272): 1057–154.

———. 1998. "City Services." *New York University Law Review* 73(1): 23.

———. 1999. *City Making*. Princeton, N.J.: Princeton University Press.

Gardner, Matthew. 1999. *The Relative Incidence of Property and Sales Taxes in North Carolina*. Washington, D.C.: Institute on Taxation and Economic Policy.

Giertz, J. Fred, and Therese McGuire. 1991. "State and Local Imposed Centralization and Local Fiscal Outcomes." In *Proceedings of the Eighty-Third Annual Conference on Taxation*, edited by Frederick Stock. Columbus, Ohio: National Tax Association.

Gillette, Clayton P. 1996. "Reconstructing Local Law of School Finance: A Cautionary Note." *Capital University Law Review* 25(37).

Goldberg, Lenny. 2000. "The Empire Has No Clothes: Infrastructure, Sprawl, Local Government Finance, and the Property Tax." *State Tax Notes* (October 2): 899–905.

Goldsmith, Mike. 1997. "Autonomy and City Limits." In *Theories of Urban Politics*, edited by David Judge, Gerry Stoker, and Harold Wolman (228–52). Thousand Oaks, Calif.: Sage Publications.

Goldsmith, Stephen. 1997. *The Twenty-First Century City*. Washington, D.C.: Regnery.

Goodspeed, Timothy J. 1998. "Tax Competition, Benefit Taxes, and Fiscal Federalism." *National Tax Journal* 51(3): 579–86.

Gramlich, Edward M. 1993. "A Policymaker's Guide to Fiscal Decentralization." *National Tax Journal* 46(2): 229–35.

Graves, Harold, ed. 1948. *Viewpoints on Public Finance*. New York: Henry Holt.

Green, Harry A., Stan Chevrin, and Cliff Lippard. 2002. "The Local Property Tax in Tennessee." *State Tax Notes* (May 27): 851–77.

Grieson, Ronald E. 1980. "Theoretical Analysis and Empirical Measurements of the Effects of the Local Income Tax." *Journal of Urban Economics* 8(1): 123–37.

Grossman, Philip J., Panayiotis Mavros, and Robert W. Wassmer. 1999. "Public Sector Technical Inefficiency in Large U.S. Cities." *Journal of Urban Economics* 46: 278–99.

Gu, Anthony Yangxiang, and Joseph Trefzger. 2000. "Make It Simple and Light: Some Thoughts on Real Estate Taxation in China." *International Real Estate Review* 3(1): 142–61.

Hamilton, Bruce W. 1975. "Zoning and Property Taxation in a System of Local Government." *Urban Studies* 12(June): 205–11.

Hansen, Susan. 1983. *The Politics of Taxation: Taxation without Representation*. New York: Praeger.

Harris, C. Lowell. 1974. *Property Taxation in Government Finance*. New York: Tax Foundation.

Haselhoff, Kim DeFronzo. 2002. "Motivations for the San Fernando Valley Succession Movement." *Journal of Urban Affairs* 24(4): 425–43.

Hassell, Daniel C. 2000. "Public Utility Real Estate Tax in Pennsylvania." *State Tax Notes* (April 10): 1301–8.

Hawkins, Richard. 2002. "The Local Revenue Roller Coaster: Growth and Stability Implications for Increasing Local Sales Tax Reliance in Georgia." Fiscal Research Project. Atlanta: Andrew Young School of Policy Studies, Georgia State University.

Hill, Steve. 2002. *Chartbook on Taxes in Maryland*. Silver Spring: Maryland Budget and Tax Policy Institute.

Hirschman, Albert O. 1970. *Exit, Voice, and Loyalty*. Cambridge: Harvard University Press.

Holcombe, Randall G. 1998. "Tax Policy from a Public Choice Perspective." *National Tax Journal* 51(2): 359–71.

Holcombe, Randall G., and Russell S. Sobel. 1997. *Growth and Variability in State Tax Revenue: An Anatomy of State Fiscal Crises*. Westport, Conn.: Greenwood Press.

Hope, Heather. 1994. "GATT May Disrupt Balance of Free Trade and Federalism, Says MTC's Bucks." *State Tax Notes* (January 17): 157.

Hoxby, Caroline M. 1995. "Does Competition among Public Schools Benefit Students and Taxpayers? Evidence from Natural Variation in School Districting." Working Paper No. 4979. Cambridge, Mass.: National Bureau of Economic Research.

———. 1998. "All Public School Finance Equalizations Are Not Created Equal." Working Paper No. 6323. Cambridge, Mass.: National Bureau of Economic Research.

Husted, Thomas A., and Lawrence Kenny. 1997. "Efficiency in Education: Evidence from the States." *1996 Proceedings of the Eighty-Ninth Annual Conference on Taxation*. Washington, D.C.: National Tax Association.

Inman, Robert, and Daniel L. Rubinfeld. 1997. "The Political Economy of Federalism." In *Perspectives on Public Choice: A Handbook*, edited by Dennis C. Mueller (73–105). Cambridge: Cambridge University Press.

Jung, Changhoon. 2001. "Does the Local Option Sales Tax Provide Property Tax Relief? The Georgia Case." *Public Budgeting and Finance* 21(1): 73–86.

Katz, Ellis. 1999. *Local Self-Government in the United States*. Washington, D.C.: United States Information Agency, United States Department of State.

Kelly, Janet, and Bruce Ransom. 2000. "State Urban Policy: 'New' Federalism in New Jersey, Virginia, and Florida." *Policy Studies Review* 17(2/3): 62–83.

Kenyon, Daphne, and John Kincaid, eds. 1991. *Competition among State and Local Governments*. Washington, D.C.: Urban Institute Press.

Kidd, Bill. 2002. "Texas House Report Criticizes Property Tax Appraisals." *State Tax Today* (August 20): 162.18.

Kincaid, John, and Richard L. Cole. 2001. "Changing Public Attitudes on Power and Taxation in the American Federal System." *Publius* 31(3): 205–14.

Knapp, John L. 1999. *Important State-Local Government Fiscal Issues*. Charlottesville, Va.: Weldon Cooper Center for Public Service.

Kuttner, Robert. 1980. *The Revolt of the Haves*. New York: Simon & Schuster.

Ladd, Helen. 1998. *Local Government Tax and Land Use Policies in the United States*. Northampton, Mass.: Edward Elgar.

Ladd, Helen, and John Yinger. 1989. *America's Ailing Cities: Fiscal Health and the Design of Urban Policy*. Baltimore: Johns Hopkins University Press.

Leland, Pamela. 2002. "PILOTs: The Large-City Experience." In *Property-Tax Exemption for Charities*, edited by Evelyn Brody (193–210). Washington, D.C.: Urban Institute Press.

Levine, Charles, and Paul L. Posner. 1981. "The Centralizing Effects of Austerity on the Intergovernmental System." *Political Science Quarterly* 96(1): 61–85.

Lewis, Paul. 2001. "Retail Politics: Local Sales Tax and the Fiscalization of Land Use." *Economic Development Quarterly* 15(1): 21–35.

Liner, Charles D. 1992. "Alternative Revenue Sources for Local Governments." *Popular Government* (winter): 22–28.

Liou, Tom Kuotsai. 1999. "Symposium on Local Economic Development Financing: Issues and Findings." *Journal of Public Budgeting, Accounting, and Financial Management* 11(fall): 386–97.

Lowery, David. 1982. "Public Choice When Services Are Costs: The Divergent Case of Assessment Administration." *American Journal of Political Science* 26(6): 57–76.

MacManus, Susan A. 1999. "Politics and Taxation." In *Handbook on Taxation*, edited by W. Bartley Hildreth and James A. Richardson (31–69). New York: Marcel Dekker, Inc.

Matsusaka, John. 1998. "Fiscal Effects of the Voter Initiative in the First Half of the Twentieth Century." *Journal of Law and Economics* 43(2): 619–50.

McCabe, Barbara Coyle, and Richard Feiock. 2000. "State Rules and Fiscal Choices." Paper presented at the annual meeting of the American Political Science Association, Washington, D.C., Aug. 31–Sept. 3.

McGuire, Therese. 1995. *Issues and Challenges in State and Local Finance*. Washington, D.C.: The Finance Project.

———. 1999. "Proposition 13 and Its Offspring: For Good or Evil?" *National Tax Journal* 52(1): 129–38.

———. 2001. "Alternatives to Property Taxation for Local Governments." In *Property Taxation and Local Government Finance*, edited by Wallace E. Oates (301–34). Cambridge, Mass.: Lincoln Institute of Land Policy.

McKinnon, Ronald, and Thomas Nechyba. 1997. "Competition in Federal Systems: The Role of Political and Financial Restraints." In *The New Federalism: Can the States Be Trusted?*, edited by John Ferejohn and Barry R. Weingast (3–61). Stanford, Calif.: Hoover Institution Press.

McLure, Charles E. 2001. "SSTP: Out of the Great Swamp, But Whither? A Plea to Rationalize the State Sales Tax." *State Tax Notes* (December 31): 1077–85.

McLure, Charles E., and Walter Hellerstein. 2002. "Does Sales-Only Apportionment of Corporate Income Violate International Trade Rules?" *State Tax Notes* (September 9): 779–86.

Micheli, Chris. 2001. "Taxable and Exempt Property in California." *State Tax Notes* (December 24): 1021–25.

Mields, Hugh. 1993. "The Property Tax: Local Revenue Mainstay." *Intergovernmental Prospective* (summer): 16–19.

Mieszkowski, Peter, and George Zodrow. 1989. "Taxation and the Tiebout Model: The Differential Effects of Head Taxes, Taxes on Land Rents, and Property Taxes." *Journal of Economic Literature* 27(3): 1098–146.

Mikesell, John L. 1993. *City Finances, City Futures*. Washington, D.C.: National League of Cities.

———. 1998. "The Future of American Sales and Use Taxation." In *The Future of State Taxation*, edited by David Brunori (15–32). Washington, D.C.: Urban Institute Press.

Minnesota Taxpayers Association. 2001. *50 State Property Tax Comparison Study*. Minneapolis: Minnesota Taxpayers Association.

Molotch, Harvey. 1976. "The City as a Growth Machine: Toward a Political Economy of Place." *The American Journal of Sociology* 82(2): 309–32.

Monkkonen, Eric H. 1995. *The Local State: Public Money and American Cities*. Stanford, Calif.: Stanford University Press.

Murray, Sheila, William Evans, and Robert M. Schwab. 1998. "Education-Finance Reform and the Distribution of Education Resources." *American Economic Review* 88(4): 789–812.

Musgrave, Richard. 1983. "Who Should Tax Where and What?" In *Tax Assignment in Federal Countries*, edited by Charles E. McLure (2–19). Canberra: Australian National University Press.

National Conference of State Legislatures (NCSL). 1992. *Principles of a High Quality State Revenue System*, 2d ed. Washington, D.C.: National Conference of State Legislatures.

————. 1997a. *Critical Issues in State-Local Fiscal Policy, A Guide to Local Option Taxes*. Denver: National Conference of State Legislatures.

————. 1997b. *Critical Issues in State-Local Fiscal Policy, Sorting Out State and Local Responsibilities*. Denver: National Conference of State Legislatures.

National League of Cities. 1998. *Major Factors Facing America's Cities*. Washington, D.C.: National League of Cities.

NCSL. See National Conference of State Legislatures.

Nechyba, Thomas J. 1997. "Local Property and State Income Taxes: The Role of Interjurisdictional Competition and Collusion." *Journal of Political Economy* 105(2): 351–84

Nechyba, Thomas, and Robert Strauss. 1998. "Community Choice and Local Public Services, Regional Science and Urban Economics." Working Paper No. 5966. Cambridge, Mass.: National Bureau of Economic Research.

Netzer, Dick. 1966. *The Economics of the Property Tax*. Washington, D.C.: Brookings Institution.

————. 1993. "Property Taxes: Their Past, Present, and Future Place in Government Finance." In *Urban Finance under Siege*, edited by Thomas Swartz and Frank Bonello (51–78). Armonk, N.Y.: M. E. Sharpe.

————. 2001. "Local Property Taxation in Theory and Practice." In *Property Taxation and Local Government Finance*, edited by Wallace E. Oates (321–38). Cambridge, Mass.: Lincoln Institute of Land Policy.

————. 2002. "Local Government Finance and the Economics of Property-Tax Exemption." In *Property-Tax Exemption for Charities*, edited by Evelyn Brody (47–80). Washington, D.C.: Urban Institute Press.

Neubig, Thomas S., and Satya Poddar. 2000. "Blurred Tax Boundaries: The New Economy's Implications for Tax Policy." *State Tax Notes* (October 9): 965–73.

Nice, David C., and Patricia Fredericksen. 1998. *The Politics of Intergovernmental Relations*. Chicago: Nelson-Hall Publishers.

Norris, Donald F. 2001. "Prospects for Regional Governance under the New Regionalism: Economic Imperatives versus Political Impediments." *Journal of Urban Affairs* 25(5): 557–72.

O'Sullivan, Arthur. 2000. "Limitations on Local Property Taxation: The U.S. Experience." *State Tax Notes* (May 15): 1697–713.

Oakland, William. 1994. "Fiscal Equalization: An Empty Box?" *National Tax Journal* 47(1): 199–209.

Oakland, William H., and William A. Testa. 1995. "Does Business Development Raise Taxes?" Federal Reserve Bank of Boston *Economic Perspective* (March/April): 22–31.

Oates, Wallace E. 1972. *Fiscal Federalism.* New York: Harcourt, Brace, Jovanovich.

———. 1979. "Lump-Sum Intergovernmental Grants Have Price Effects." In *Fiscal Federalism and Grants-in-Aid,* edited by Peter Mieszkowski and William Oakland (23–30). Washington, D.C.: Urban Institute Press.

———. 1991. "The Theory and Rationale of Local Property Taxation." In *State and Local Finance for the 1990s,* edited by Dana Wolf Naimark and Therese McGuire. Tempe: Arizona State University.

———. 1993. "Fiscal Decentralization and Economic Development." *National Tax Journal* 46(2): 237–43.

———. 1999a. "An Essay on Fiscal Federalism." *Journal of Economic Literature* 37(3): 1120–49.

———. 1999b. "Local Property Taxation: An Assessment." *Assessment Journal* (September): 67–69.

———. 2001a. "Property Taxation and Local Government Finance." In *Property Taxation and Local Government Finance,* edited by Wallace E. Oates (21–32). Cambridge, Mass.: Lincoln Institute of Land Policy.

———, ed. 2001b. *Property Taxation and Local Government Finance.* Cambridge, Mass.: Lincoln Institute of Land Policy.

Oates, Wallace E., and Robert M. Schwab. 1997. "The Impact of Urban Land Taxation: The Pittsburgh Experience." *National Tax Journal* 50(1): 1–21.

Oliver, J. Eric. 2000. "City Size and Civic Involvement in Metropolitan America." *American Political Science Review* 94(2): 361–94.

Ostrom, Elinor. 1983. "The Social Stratification-Government Inequality Thesis Explored." *Urban Affairs Quarterly* 19(1): 91–112.

Pagano, Michael. 2002. *City Fiscal Conditions in 2002.* Washington, D.C.: National League of Cities.

Pagano, Michael, and Richard Forgette. 2001. "Fiscal Structure and Metropolitan Tax Base Sharing." Paper presented at the American Political Science Association annual meeting, San Francisco, Sept. 1.

Paget, Karen. 1998. "Can Cities Escape Political Isolation?" *American Prospect* 10 (January 2): 2.

Pammer, William. 1996. "Economic Development Strategies among Counties." In *The American County: Frontiers of Knowledge,* edited by Donald E. Menzel (184–202). Tuscaloosa: University of Alabama Press.

Papke, James A. 2000. "Rethinking Local Business Taxation: Substituting a State Value-Added Tax for the Local Ad Valorem Tax on Business Personal Property." *State Tax Notes* (February 28): 669–82.

Park, Keeok. 1996. "Determination of County Government Growth." In *The American County: Frontiers of Knowledge,* edited by Donald Menzel (34–52). Tuscaloosa: University of Alabama Press.

———. 1997. "Friends and Competitors: Policy Interactions between Local Governments in Metropolitan Areas." *Political Research Quarterly* 50(4): 723–50.

Parks, Roger B., and Elinor Ostrom. 1981. "Complex Models of Urban Service Systems." In *Urban Policy Analysis: Directions for Future Research,* edited by Terry Clark (171–99). Thousand Oaks, Calif.: Sage Publications.

Percy, Stephen, Brett W. Hawkins, and Peter E. Maier. 1995. "Revisiting Tiebout: Moving Rationales and Interjurisdictional Relocation." *Publius* 25(4): 117.

Peterson, George E. 1994. *Big-City Politics, Governance, and Fiscal Constraints.* Washington, D.C.: Urban Institute Press.

Peterson, Paul E. 1981. *City Limits.* Chicago: University of Chicago Press.

———. 1995a. *The Price of Federalism.* Washington, D.C.: Brookings Institution.

———. 1995b. "Who Should Do What?" *The Brookings Review* (spring): 6–11.

Peterson, Paul E., and Mark Rom. 1989. "American Federalism, Welfare Policy and Relocation Choices." *American Political Science Review* 83(3): 711–28.

Pogue, Thomas F. 1998. "State and Local Business Taxation: Principles and Prospects." In *The Future of State Taxation*, edited by David Brunori (89–110). Washington, D.C.: Urban Institute Press.

Pomp, Richard. 2002. "The Collision between Nonprofits and Cities over the Property Tax: Possible Solutions." In *Property-Tax Exemption for Charities*, edited by Evelyn Brody (383–91). Washington, D.C.: Urban Institute Press.

Poterba, James M., and Kim S. Rueben. 1995. "The Effects of Property Limits on Wages and Employment in the Local Public Sector." *American Economic Review* 85(2): 384–89.

Preston, Anne E., and Casey Ichniowski. 1992. "A National Perspective on the Nature and Effects of the Local Property Tax Revolt, 1976–1986." *National Tax Journal* 44(2): 123–45.

Rafool, Mandy. 2002. *A Guide to Property Taxes: An Assessment.* Washington, D.C.: National Conference of State Legislatures.

Reese, Thomas. 1980. *The Politics of Taxation.* Westport, Conn.: Quorum Books.

Report of the Commission on Virginia's State and Local Tax Structure for the 21st Century. 2000 (December). Commonwealth of Virginia.

Reschovsky, Andrew. 1993. "Are City Fiscal Crises on the Horizon?" In *Urban Finance under Siege*, edited by Thomas Swartz and Frank Bonello (107–37). Armonk, N.Y.: M. E. Sharpe.

———. 1994. *Do the Elderly Face High Property Tax Burdens?* Washington, D.C.: American Association of Retired Persons.

Richman, Roger. 2002. "Local Government, Federalism, and the Telecommunications Revolution." *State and Local Government Review* 34(2): 133–44.

Rubin, Irene S. 1998. *Class, Tax, and Power: Municipal Budgeting in the United States.* Chatham, N.J.: Chatham House.

Rymarowicz, Lillian, and Dennis Zimmerman. 1988. "Federal Budget and Tax Policy and the State-Local Sector: Retrenchment in the 1980s." Washington, D.C.: Congressional Research Service.

Schmarr, John, and Nikki Spretnak. 2000. "Ohio's Municipal Tax System—Modernizing a Fifty-Year-Old Taxing System." *State Tax Notes* (October 9): 975–82.

Schneider, Mark. 1986. "Fragmentation and the Growth of Local Government." *Public Choice* 48(1): 255–64.

———. 1989. *The Competitive City: The Political Economy of Suburbia.* Pittsburgh: University of Pittsburgh Press.

Schwab, Robert, and Amy Rehder Harris. 1998. *An Analysis of the Graded Property Tax, in Taxing Simply, Taxing Fairly.* Washington, D.C.: District of Columbia Tax Revision Commission.

Sexton, Terri A., and Steven M. Sheffrin. 1995. "Five Lessons from Tax Revolts." *State Tax Notes* (December 18): 1763–68.

Sexton, Terri A., Steven M. Sheffrin, and Arthur O'Sullivan. 1999. "Proposition 13: Unintended Effects and Feasible Reforms." *National Tax Journal* 52(1): 99–112.

Shadbegian, Ronald J. 1998. "Do Tax and Expenditure Limitations Affect Local Government Budgets? Evidence from Panel Data." *Public Finance Review* 26(2): 218–36.

———. 1999. "The Effect of Tax and Expenditure Limitations on the Revenue Structure of Local Government, 1962–87." *National Tax Journal* 52(2): 221–38.

Shaviro, Daniel. 1993. *Federalism in Taxation.* Washington, D.C.: AEI Press.

Sheffrin, Steven M. 1998. "The Future of the Property Tax: A Political Economy Perspective." In *The Future of State Taxation,* edited by David Brunori (129–45). Washington, D.C.: Urban Institute Press.

———. 1999. "Interview: Steven M. Sheffrin, on the Worst Tax, Local Options, and Proposition 13." *State Tax Notes* (December 19): 1721–23.

Shoup, Carl. 1937. *Facing the Tax Problem.* New York: Twentieth Century Fund.

Shuford, Gordon, and Richard Young. 2000. *A Report on Local Government Funding: An Overview of National Issues and Trends.* Columbia: University of South Carolina.

Silva, Fabio, and Jon Sonstelie. 1995. "Did Serrano Cause a Decline in School Spending?" *National Tax Journal* 48(2): 199–215.

Sjoquist, David L. 1982. "The Effect of the Number of Local Governments on Central City Expenditures." *National Tax Journal* 37(1): 79–88.

Slemrod, Joel. 1995. "Professional Opinions about Tax Policy." *National Tax Journal* 48(1): 121–47.

Sobel, Russell S. 1997. "Optimal Taxation in a Federal System of Government." *Southern Economic Journal* 64(2): 468–85.

Sokolow, Alvin D. 1998. "The Changing Property Tax and State and Local Relations." *Publius* 28(1): 165–87.

———. 2000. "The Changing Property Tax in the West: State Centralization of Local Finance." *Public Budget and Finance* 20(1): 85–104.

Steinberg, Richard, and Mark Bilodeau. 1999. *Should Non-Profit Organizations Pay Sales or Property Tax?* Washington, D.C.: National Council of Nonprofit Associations.

Steuerle, Eugene. 1991. *The Tax Decade: How Taxes Came to Dominate the Public Agenda.* Washington, D.C.: Urban Institute Press.

Stevens, G. Ross. 1974. "State Centralization and the Erosion of Local Autonomy." *Journal of Politics* 36: 44–76.

Stone, Clarence. 1989. *Regime Politics: Governing Atlanta, 1946–1988.* Lawrence: University of Kansas Press.

Stone, Clarence, and Heywood Sanders. 1987. "Development Policies Reconsidered." *Urban Affairs Quarterly* 22(4): 521–39.

Strauss, Robert. 1995. "Reducing New York's Reliance on the School Property Tax." *State Tax Notes* (July 31): 339–60.

———. 1997. "Why Homeowners Hate the Local Property Tax." *State Tax Notes* (June 16): 1802–6.

———. 2001. "Pennsylvania's Local Property Tax." *State Tax Notes* (June 4): 1963–83.

Strauss, Robert, and Tomohiro Nakamura. 1999. "The Income and Household Composition of City-County Migrants in the 1990s." *State Tax Notes* (February 1): 327–37.

Stull, William, and Judith Stull. 1991. "Capitalization of Local Income Taxes." *Journal of Urban Economics* 29(2): 182–90.

Swain, John. 2000. "The Taxation of Private Interests in Public Property: Toward a Unified Approach." *Utah Law Review* 3(1): 421–82.

Swanstrom, Todd. 1985. *The Crisis of Growth Politics*. Philadelphia: Temple University Press.

———. 2001. "What We Argue about When We Argue about Regionalism." *Journal of Urban Affairs* 23(5): 479–96.

Swartz, Thomas R., and Frank J. Bonello. 1993. *Urban Finance under Siege*. Armonk, N.Y.: M.E. Sharpe

Tannenwald, Robert. 2002. "Are State and Local Revenue Systems Becoming Obsolete?" *State Tax Notes* (April 8): 143–59.

Teske, Paul, Mark Schneider, Michael Mintrom, and Samuel Best. 1993. "Establishing the Micro Foundations of a Macro Theory: Information, Movers, and the Competitive Local Market for Public Goods." *American Political Science Review* 87(3): 702–13.

Theobald, Neil D., and Lawrence O. Picus. 1991. "Living with Equal Amounts of Less: Experience of States with Primarily State Funded School Systems." *Journal of Education Finance* 17(summer): 1–6.

Thomas, John P. 1991. "Financing County Government: An Overview." *Intergovernmental Perspective* 17(winter): 10–13.

Thomas, Kenneth. 2000. *Competing for Capital: Europe and North America in a Global Era*. Washington, D.C.: Georgetown University Press.

Thomas, Robert. 1986. "Cities as Partners in the Federal System." *Political Science Quarterly* 101(1): 49–64.

Tiebout, Charles M. 1956. "A Pure Theory of Local Expenditures." *Journal of Political Economics* 64 (October): 416–24.

Tuerck, David G., Jonathan Haughton, Corina Murg, and Sorin Codreanu. 2001. *Tax Changes in New York City, The New York City Tax Analysis Modeling Program*. Boston: Beacon Hill Institute at Suffolk University.

U.S. Census Bureau. 1992. State tax data. Washington, D.C.: Government Printing Office.

———. 1993. State tax data. Washington, D.C.: Government Printing Office.

———. 1998. State tax data. Washington, D.C.: Government Printing Office.

———. 2000. State tax data. Washington, D.C.: Government Printing Office.

———. 2002. State tax data. Washington, D.C.: Government Printing Office.

Veasey, R. Lawson, and Ronn Hy. 2000. "Heaven or Hell? What Fate Awaits Post–Property Tax Arkansas." *Arkansas Business and Economics Review* 33(1): 2–10.

Vickrey, William. 1970. "Defining Land Values for Tax Purposes." In *The Assessment of Land Value*, edited by Daniel Holland (25–36). Madison: University of Wisconsin Press.

Vitaliano, Donald, F. 1999. "Property Tax, Farm." In *The Encyclopedia of Taxation and Tax Policy*, edited by Joseph Cordes, Robert Ebel, and Jane Gravelle (287–89). Washington, D.C.: Urban Institute Press.

Wallace, Sally, and Barbara M. Edwards. 1999. "Personal Income Tax." In *Handbook on Taxation*, edited by W. Bartley Hildreth and James A. Richardson (149–90). New York: Marcel Dekker, Inc.

Wallis, John Joseph. 2001. "A History of the Property Tax in America." In *Property Taxation and Local Government Finance*, edited by Wallace E. Oates (123–47). Cambridge, Mass.: Lincoln Institute of Land Policy.

Walters, Lawrence C., and Gary C. Cornia 1997. "The Implications of Utility and Telecommunications Deregulation for Local Finance." *State and Local Government Review* 29(3): 172–87.

———. 2001. "Electric Utility Deregulation and School Finance in the United States." *Journal of Education Finance* 26(4): 345–72.

Walters, Lawrence C., Gary C. Cornia, and David W. Shank. 1995. "Appraisal of Public Utilities and Railroads for Ad Valorem Taxation: Procedural and Technical Overview." *State Tax Notes* (May 29): 2231–41.

Wassmer, Robert W. 1998. "Local Financing Options for Urban Governments." *State Tax Notes* (January 19): 197–200.

Wassmer, Robert W., and Ronald C. Fisher. 2000. "Tiebout, Time, and Transition in the Structure of Local Government in U.S. Metropolitan Areas." Working Paper. Available from the Social Science Research Network, http://www.papers.ssrn.com.

Wayslenko, Michael. 1986. "Local Tax Policy and Industry Location: A Review of the Evidence." In *1985 Proceedings of the 78th Annual Conference on Taxation*, edited by Stanley J. Bowers and Janet L. Stanton. Washington, D.C.: National Tax Association.

Wilgoren, Debbie. 2002. "Even Poor Back Revitalization, Poll Finds." *Washington Post*, 1 July, B-1.

Wolman, Harold. 1988. "Local Economic Development Policy: What Explains the Divergence between Policy Analysis and Political Behavior?" *Journal of Urban Affairs* 6(1): 151–80.

———. 1997. "Local Government Institutions and Democratic Governance." In *Theories of Urban Politics*, edited by David Judge, Gerry Stoker, and Harold Wolman (135–59). Thousand Oaks, Calif.: Sage Publications.

Woodwell, James. 1998. *Major Factors Affecting American Cities*. Washington, D.C.: National League of Cities.

Yates, Douglas. 1984. *The Ungovernable City*. Boston: MIT Press.

Youngman, Joan M. 1996. "States of Mind: Alternatives for Property Tax Revision and Reform." *State Tax Notes* (July 29): 303–6.

———. 1997a. "States of Mind: Property Taxes and the 1997 Elections." *State Tax Notes* (December 22): 1619–21.

———. 1997b. "States of Mind: P.S. 41, School Finance, and the Property Tax." *State Tax Notes* (November 3): 1116–18.

———. 1998a. "Property, Taxes, and the Future of Property Taxes." In *The Future of State Taxation*, edited by David Brunori (111–27). Washington, D.C.: Urban Institute Press.

———. 1998b. "States of Mind: Tax Incentives and Tax Policy, a Property Tax Perspective." *State Tax Notes* (March 16): 849–53.

———. 1999a. "Property Taxes in an Age of Globalization." *State Tax Notes* (June 7): 1897–900.

———. 1999b. "States of Mind: The Hardest Challenge for Value-Based Property Taxes: Part I." *State Tax Notes* (March 8): 745–48.

————.1999c. "States of Mind: The Hardest Challenge for Value-Based Property Taxes: Part II. *State Tax Notes* (April 26): 1393–97.

————. 2000. "States of Mind: Causes of Controversy in Property Tax Exemption Cases." *State Tax Notes* (January 3): 45–49.

————. 2002a. "Enlarging the Property Tax Debate—Regressivity and Fairness." *State Tax Notes* (October 7): 45–52.

————. 2002b. "Expanding the Property Tax Debate—Tax Impacts on First-Time Homebuyers and Senior Citizens." *State Tax Notes* (March 25): 1057–62.

Zodrow, George. 2001. "Reflections on the New View and the Benefit View of the Property Tax." In *Property Taxation and Local Government Finance*, edited by Wallace E. Oates (79–112). Cambridge, Mass.: Lincoln Institute of Land Policy.

About the Author

David Brunori is a journalist, author, educator, and lawyer who specializes in tax and government issues. He is a frequent speaker at conferences around the United States on the subject of state and local tax policy. Brunori is contributing editor for *State Tax Notes* magazine and the author of *The Politics of State Taxation,* a weekly column focusing on state tax and budget policies. He is a research professor of public policy at The George Washington University and teaches state and local tax at the law school. Previously he served as a trial attorney with the U.S. Department of Justice and practiced law with a Washington, D.C., law firm. He wrote *State Tax Policy: A Political Perspective* and edited *The Future of State Taxation* (both published by the Urban Institute Press), and has published articles in the *National Tax Journal* and the *State and Local Government Review.* He earned bachelor's and master's degrees from The George Washington University and his law degree from the University of Pittsburgh School of Law. He is currently a David C. Lincoln Fellow at the Lincoln Institute of Land Policy.

Index

aging population, 12, 120–121
allocative services, 32
antitaxation, raising revenue in era of,
    39–41
autonomy
    challenges to political, 123–126
    fiscal, 22–24
        need for, 4
    under siege, 4, 25–26
    local government, 4, 15–16
    recommendations for strengthening
        local tax, 126–138

benefits principle, 42–43
Bird, Richard M., 22–24, 43, 97
business income taxes, local-option, 94
business personal property taxes, 95–96
    problems posed by, 96
business taxes. *See* local-option business
    taxes

California, 138
charitable exemptions, 63–64, 70n.9
cigarette taxes, 82–83
commuters, taxing, 90–91
competition, 11, 19, 20, 131
    with foreign nations, 115–116

harmful, 37–38, 94, 131–132
corporate income taxes. *See* local-option
    business income taxes

decentralization, 26n.1, 104–105
democratic ideals and practices, 3–4,
    21–22
demographic changes, 12
deregulation, 12, 119–120

economic development exemptions, 63
economy
    raising revenue in the modern, 11–12
    tax policy in the new, 121–122
education. *See* school finance
electoral tax politics, 30
electric utilities. *See* utilities
electronic commerce, 76, 117–118
excise taxes, 8, 9
exempt properties, 13
exemption(s). *See also* property tax,
    exemptions
    charitable, 63–64, 70n.9
    economic development, 63
    government property, 64–65
    homestead, 65–66
    for nonprofit organizations, 132